THE WINNING FEELING:

A Program to Successfully Develop Self-Esteem

by
JOHN R. KEARNS, Ph.D.
and
GARRY SHULMAN, Ph.D.

R&E Publishers
Saratoga, California

Copyright © 1994 by John R. Kearns, Ph.D. and Garry Shulman, Ph.D.

This book is sold with the understanding that the subject matter covered herein is of a general nature and does not constitute professional advice for any specific individual or situation. Anyone planning to take action in any of the areas that this book describes should, of course, seek professional advice as would be prudent and advisable under their given circumstances.

R & E Publishers
P.O. Box 2008, Saratoga, CA 95070
Tel: (408) 866-6303   Fax: (408) 866-0825

Book Design by Diane Parker

Cover by Kaye Quinn

Kearns, John R.
    The winning feeling: a program to successfully develop self-esteem / by John R. Kearns and Garry Shulman.
        p.   cm.
    Includes bibliographical references.
    ISBN 1-56875-060-9 $9.95
    1. Self-esteem. I. Shulman, Garry. II. Title.
BF697.5.S46K43   1993
158'.1--dc20   93-23365
                                                  CIP

Introduction

Success! Ah, the time and energy that we devote to its pursuit! All the study time; all the time on task; all the long hours of planning. Are we our own masters? Or is the outcome of our efforts largely predetermined by some series of events of which we may be unaware?

In today's society there are few issues in which we all share a common feeling or belief. One area however, in which all parents are united in a bond of concern is in the feelings we share for our children. Nothing is more dominant in our thoughts than the secured safety of our young, the health and welfare of our young, and the ultimate success and happiness of our young.

While this wish for the success and happiness of those who are dearest to us is a heartfelt desire, we also share the feeling of helplessness in being able to guarantee this state for our children. How do we provide for success for our children? Or can we? What is happiness? What can we do as parents to ensure that our children will ultimately live happy and productive lives?

These questions are difficult if not impossible for most to address let alone to answer in satisfactory, concrete terms.

From countless research studies that have been conducted on the lives of top performing people in various walks of life, we know that happy and successful people share certain qualities and characteristics. Whether the studies have examined people in athletics or business, in sales or in the medical profession, people who describe themselves as happy and successful have had a feeling of being in control of the decisions that effect their lives. They also had the confidence in their ability to make informed decisions and feel good about them. They have had positive self-esteem and a sense of direction.

Positive self-esteem is not something that one is born with...it cannot be acquired. It doesn't come as the result of good breeding or a specific social class or the success of a particular family. Instead, self-esteem is developed. It begins on the day of our birth. Throughout our childhood, we have countless interactions with various people. Our parents and relatives, our coaches and teachers, and our friends all play an important role in helping us to develop our image of who we believe ourselves to be. Over time, we come to perceive ourselves as responsible, capable, valuable and loveable. Hopefully this is the outcome. Yet the truth is, that for many children the view that they develop of themselves is exactly the opposite. Too often children learn to believe that they are incapable of dealing with life's situations. They learn to believe that their value as a member in a class or a family is inconsequential...that they don't matter to those around them.

When a belief develops that one is incapable, irresponsible or of little value, the individual who has this belief acts as if it were true. If a student believes that he cannot do mathematics, he will approach mathematics with a predetermined belief that he will not be successful. If a child believes that he cannot hit a ball in baseball, the predetermined belief interferes with that child being successful in hitting the ball. In fact, the limitations that we find in life are not so much a factor of what we are, but more importantly what we think we are not. Think about that for a minute...it is not what we are that holds us back, it is what we think we are not!

So as parents we must ask the question, "How can I ensure that my child will be successful?" "How can I ensure that my child will see the world as a place full of possibilities and challenges waiting to be conquered?" "How can I ensure that my child will see herself in a positive light?"

To draw upon a parallel incident from the animal world might serve as an example to help clarify this point. Circus trainers are often forced to deal with both mature and young elephants simultaneously. On one such occasion, a young boy was walking by and noticed that tied to a telephone pole were two elephants, a full grown female and baby elephant approximately four months of age.

The boy noticed that the mother elephant was secured by only a small rope while tied to the same pole, heavy leg irons and a substantial chain held the baby elephant. The boy noticed too, that the mother was typically quite passive. The baby was pulling on the chain, all the time trying to free itself from its restriction.

The boy asked the trainer why the elephants were secured in this manner. The trainer answered that the mother elephant had learned over the years that no matter how hard she tried to become free, it was not to be. The baby elephant had not yet learned that it could not become free and so, was still fighting to free itself. That is why the heavier leg iron was still required.

The paradox, of course is, that even though the physical size of the mother elephant had changed, and breaking free from the little rope would be a very simple matter, she believed that she could not. Irrespective of what the facts of the matter were, her belief in her inability to get free prevented her from making the attempt.

And so it is with people. Irrespective of the truth of the situation that we may find ourselves in, we respond to the situation based on our belief structure of our abilities or our inabilities. Our self-concept is a major controlling factor in our behavior and determines to a large extent our success in life.

So to address the question of insuring our children's well being...what can be said? Success breeds success...an old adage, yes but so true none-the-less. Our inner drive to pursue new challenges, to address the future with a positive and optimistic set of expectations is directly related to the success that we have previously experienced in similar situations. If we provide experiences for our children that are developmentally appropriate and within their ability range, the opportunity for them to experience success dramatically increases. With the increase in success comes a personal sense that is reflected in the belief held by the child that "I am responsible and capable of dealing with what is expected of me." It is the responsibility of coaches, teachers and parents to provide opportunities for children to routinely experience situations in which success is probable. By orchestrating programs and learning experiences where this can occur, we go a long way to ensuring that our children will develop positive self-images and positive expectations about themselves.

This book will examine many techniques that have been tested in a variety of settings from business and industry to athletics and the classroom. They have been found to be effective in assisting people to stretch beyond their current level of achievement to attain new personal firsts, new personal highs. For those who already possess some positive level of self-esteem, the principles taught in this book will enhance that level. Those who unfortunately do not have adequate levels of self-esteem which limits them coming close to their potential may be helped by this program. This is a critical step in building a positive self-esteem.

Contents

1

Recognizing the Importance of Positive Self-Esteem

Maxwell Maltz, the author of *Psychocybernetics,* wrote that the discovery of the self was the most important scientific discovery of the 20th Century. Many agree with this conclusion, and yet for all the importance that people in the *people business* attribute to the self, very little is known by practitioners of how to actually build a positive self-esteem in children.

Part of the reason for this, especially in the case of education, is that the training that most teachers receive does not deal with this subject in any kind of detail. In education, it is a motherhood statement to say that positive self-esteem is important to learning. The converse is that a negative view of oneself detracts from a student's potential to learn. It would be difficult to find someone in education to argue this point.

However, while the importance of a positive self-image is a common belief in educational circles, Colleges of Education spend little time developing this phenomena and training prospective teachers in proven effective strategies to enhance the self-esteem of students.

It has been common knowledge for many years that, as a group, the academic self-esteem of students continues to decline the longer students stay in school. In a recent study (Kearns, 1987), students were asked to agree or disagree with the following statement..."My teacher makes me feel I'm not good enough." Of approximately 1500 students responding to the survey, at grade four, 28 percent of the students agreed with the statement; at grade five, 30 percent agreed with the statement; and at grade six, 36 percent of the students agreed...."My teacher makes me feel I'm not good enough."

This is incredible! After many years in various aspects of education, it has been our experience that teachers certainly do not go out of their way to give students this impression. If anything, teachers bend over backward to give students exactly the opposite impression of themselves. Yet somehow the message that is being sent out by teachers is not being received by students in the manner in which it is intended. It is also important to note, that it is not just students who are experiencing academic difficulties who agreed with the statement. Even students who excel often develop the idea that their work is not good enough.

How does this happen?

In an attempt to partially explain this phenomena, a distinction needs to be established between two terms that are often used interchangeably. The two terms are *achievement* and *accomplishment.* By way of definition, *achievement* will be used here to refer to attainment at an extremely high level. *Accomplishment,* on the other hand, will be used to refer to what a person can do, to how that person has changed in a period of time because of the work that he has put forth, because of his own good efforts.

As parents, we would love to see our children as achievers, leading the way, excelling in all that they do. We often, with only the best of intentions for our children, unconsciously apply pressure while encouraging them to strive to be the best, to be achievers. This occurs in families which have a tradition of achieving and also in families which don't have this tradition but recognize the inherent value of this level of attainment.

Teachers, collectively, are achievers academically. They have all played the academic game and won! All have university degrees, many have graduate degrees. During the many years that teachers have been involved in pursuing their own studies, a set of values has also been developed that are in keeping with the experience of working with high expectations and producing to high standards of excellence. Irrespective of the grades that individuals received during their university years, they were at least good enough to graduate. This standard alone sets teachers apart from most of North American society.

The fact is that in general, only one out of ten students in our public schools pursues a university education. Only one in ten is an achiever by this same definition.

It is human nature for people to wish to be around others who share similar values. Correspondingly, it is natural for educators to respond more positively to, and to reinforce those students who most closely reflect the teacher's values and expectations for high standards. They are the students who perform the best who routinely have their work displayed in a prominent location. They are the students who perform the best who routinely have their stories or poems published in the school newspaper. And they are the students who perform the best who routinely are being recognized by their peers and the academic staff as the best, having their sense of self bolstered in the process.

But there is a problem with devoting so much attention to those who are *the best, the winners, the achievers.* In any situation where the winners rise to the top, whether it be in sport or in academics, by definition, everyone else is a loser. Unfortunately, over many years, too many of the students in our schools have come to see themselves as just that, losers. If not losers, then certainly the image of being not good enough comes through loud and clear.

We have all experienced watching very young children learn to walk, learn to talk or learn to ride a bike. Initially, their attempts are met with many unsuccessful attempts. But they try again and again. Eventually the first step is taken or the first word spoken. The joy that accompanies these acts is displayed by both the parent and the child. These are acts of accomplishment, and they are the first acts of success that a child has experienced in a given area. The success is encouragement for the child to try again. Soon more steps are taken, but not without many skinned knees.

But amazingly, the skinned knees are forgotten and further attempts are made. And so it must be with all learning that is programmed for children. It is the establishment of a large base of accomplishment, of a large base of successful experiences that is the foundation for the development of a healthy sense of self-esteem.

If we have tried and found success, we are more likely to try again when a new challenge is in our path. Attempting the next rung up the ladder is more certain if we have experienced success in the past at the previous level. Previous successful experiences act as a psychological crash mat. If the mat is in place and secure, one is more likely to attempt the jump. In fact, the act of jumping can be pleasurable in itself, irrespective of the outcome.

As parents and teachers, we need to be aware of this psychological relationship. When beginning any new set of experiences, whether it be reading, swimming or riding a horse, children require a firm foundation of accomplishment that they can refer to as successful experiences. They need to be able to say with wonder in their voices and in their eyes, "Wow! Look what I can do!" Positive experiences that lead to this kind of self-recognition of ability tell children a lot of valuable information about themselves. They learn that they are able and capable of being successful in a given area of endeavor. This in part contributes to the development of a positive self-esteem. With this base, children will be less reluctant to take the next step which leads closer to a higher level of achievement.

A child's perception of self is critical because no matter how many successful attempts are experienced, some children still perceive themselves as being unsuccessful. To an observer, the conclusion would be that this individual is successful and should have a positive self-image. However, growing numbers of children do not feel this way, despite the evidence. They perceive themselves as being underachievers, losers, or just plain dumb. Attempts to rationally change one's perception are seldom successful.

A major component of any self-esteem program must address the emotional component of self. Self-esteem is partially rational and partially emotional. Trying to rationally convince a low esteemed student of their higher level of ability is often met by a series of, "Yeah...but," statements. This is the emotional element which allows the perception of information to be compared with what is believed to be the reality of the student. Without acknowledging the emotions which root perceptions in the subconscious, attempts to change behavior through self-concept adjustment are usually unsuccessful. This concept will be addressed in the subsequent chapters of this book.

SUMMARY CHAPTER ONE

1. Many of the learning difficulties that are experienced by children can be traced back to how children perceive themselves as learners.

2. Achievement, as used in this text, is defined as a lofty level of attainment, something that is done extremely well. Accomplishment is defined as what a person can do. The opportunity to celebrate accomplishment comes when students compare their current level of operation in any given task with where they were performing in the past. Everyone can celebrate accomplishment. Not everyone can perform at an achievement level.

2

The Development of Self-Esteem in Children

Teachers and parents alike have long recognized the importance of positive self feelings for success. To professional educators it has become common to discuss the merits of positive self-esteem in correlation with high academic achievement. Clearly, the belief within the profession is..."If students have positive self-regard, they will be able to perform better academically and socially than if they do not." In a recent study conducted by Wattenburg and Clifford, children in kindergarten were administered two standardized tests. One was a self-concept inventory and the other was an IQ test. The researchers wanted to determine which was a better predictor of future reading ability. What they discovered was, that based on the tests, the self-concept scores of young children were better predictors of reading ability three years into the future than were IQ scores.

This is startling news in light of the importance that has historically been given to intelligence in relation to success in school. Please don't misunderstand. Intelligence is very important. But in the absence of positive self-esteem, the full potential of intelligence will not be realized.

Self-esteem is one of the most important factors influencing success at school. Children with superior intelligence and low self-esteem can perform poorly at school while children with high self-esteem and *average* intelligence can succeed. Teacher comments such as, "not living up to one's potential" or, "can do better," can often be traced to how students feel about themselves. The motivation of such students is often in question by the teacher. The focus of low self-esteem students is more frequently on issues other than school tasks, such as their feelings about themselves, social relationships, their fears and anxieties, and the avoidance of risk situations that focus on their weaknesses and incompetencies.

Frequently, the experiences that lead to and reinforce low self-esteem are school related. This can produce feelings of anxiety that the child is continually forced to address. It becomes a never ending circle. Low self-esteem interferes with school performance (figure 1), and substandard performance reinforces the feelings of low self-esteem. The child comes to believe that he is a poor performer.

Children who are experiencing difficulties academically are often referred to specialists for remedial assistance. In some cases this is warranted. However, often the academic problem is a symptom of poor self-esteem. Through treatment of the symptom, progress is frequently slow, while the enhancement of the child's self-esteem is overlooked. The pattern often becomes one of continuing failure, reinforcement of the belief that, "I can't do this," and increasing self-doubt.

Increasing learner anxiety is a result which directly interferes with one's ability to focus on the task at hand. This leads to further academic frustration and low motivation to learn.

NOTHING SUCCEEDS LIKE SUCCESS!

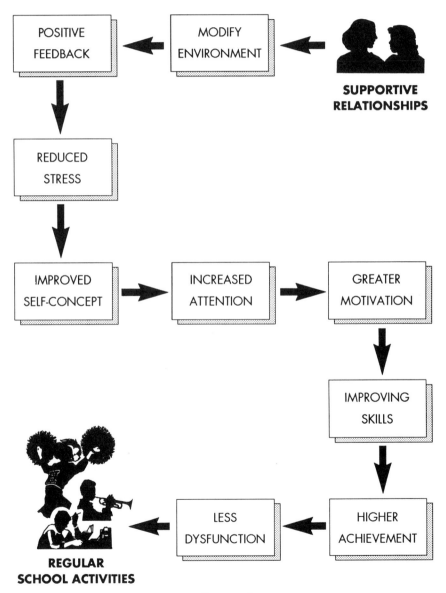

Figure 1

Self-concept is directly related to feelings that individuals have about themselves. These feelings evolve within the self and originate as a result of the many interactions that are experienced with important people in a student's life, and with the involvement that one has with events.

There is a close relationship that exists between the development of the self-concept and the development of self-confidence and a self-esteem. As adults and as children, we see our ability to be able to handle different situations vary from event to event. Our feelings of adequacy vary depending on the situation in which we find ourselves. By comparing our comfort level in the following situations, the point can be seen.

Rank yourself on a scale from one to seven in each of the following situations. *One* means that you feel very anxious and unable to comfortably deal with the event, while *Seven* means that this event is a most natural and tension free experience for you. Give yourself a score for each of the following situations, selecting any number from one to seven that represents your feeling of confidence in being able to meet the demands presented. Here are some situations:

a) preparing a Christmas meal for 20 people

b) scaling a 40 foot vertical rock wall with the assistance of safety ropes

c) driving your car on icy roads at night

d) speaking in public to 400 people

e) changing a flat tire

f) dealing with high pressure sales people

g) baking cookies

h) washing the car

If you are like most people, you will have a wide range of scores that you have assigned to these situations. This is an indication of your self-confidence to be able to respond comfortably.

Very closely linked to self-confidence is one's feelings of self-esteem, one's feelings about one's self in each of these conditions. Self-confidence is a belief that one has about one's ability to do tasks. The performance of tasks is a phenomena which is operational at the *accomplishment* level. For positive feelings and positive self-esteem to develop, one must have increasing opportunities to succeed at tasks; to be aware of one's abilities and be able to develop an attitude that says, "Look what I can do." Through increasingly challenging tasks, one has an opportunity to experience a multitude of successes and be able to see others' reactions to them. The reaction of significant others (parents, coaches and teachers, etc.) to the successes of a child will invariably be positive and encouraging. Over time, a child will begin to feel good about himself (the emotional component) and increasingly confident in his ability to take care of himself.

Self-confidence and self-esteem are related to self-concept. Self-concept is defined as the person's perception of who he is. Self-esteem on the other hand evaluates this perception in either positive or negative terms. In essence, self-esteem is the value that we place on the various dimensions of our self-concept. Self-confidence is a natural dimension that helps to form the self-concept.

We describe ourselves in terms of our roles in life, in terms of our specific abilities and in terms of our varying attributes. Our self-concept is comprised of many mental images and many dimensions.

Theorists currently believe the following to be true of the self-concept:

a) **The self-concept is multidimensional.** A general perception of our self exists which is made up of many subparts. Further, it is even possible for the subparts to be multidimensional. For example, one subpart may be our self-concept as a student. But this general descriptor can be further divided into a student of math, history, art, reading, etc.

b) **The self-concept is hierarchical.** Certain dimensions of the self are more important to describing the central perception that one holds of oneself than are others. For example, for most children, their role as students and family members holds far more importance than their role as gardeners or artists. These dimensions can change as life styles in adolescence and adulthood are selected.

c) **The self-concept is reasonably stable and consistent.** This is especially true with core values, such as the belief that youngsters hold about their abilities as students. Once core values have been established, it is very difficult to change them. What is necessary to bring about change to a central belief are many inconsistent experiences with the self-perception. Initially, an individual will choose to disregard the inconsistency as an error of some type which is unlikely to reoccur (see Chapter 8).

Children will act in a manner which confirms the view that they hold of themselves. For instance, if a child believes that he is *good*, he will make every attempt to act in a way that is consistent with this belief. Conversely, if a child sees himself as *bad*, he will unconsciously seek out criticism and punishment..."If I can't be the best, then I'll be the best at being the worst," is often what children appear to say through their behavior. Further, if a child sees himself as weak in math, the results from math assignments and tests will tend to confirm this. Any deviation from this performance will likely be explained by the student as *an easy test* or *luck*.

Even though there may be evidence to support a new belief and new forms of behavior, it is hard to accept new beliefs about the self. Psychologically, the purpose of rejecting the inconsistency is so that the self-concept can feel comfortable with its present perception.

Consistency in perception decreases the further away from core values we go (figure 2). Time, physical and social growth, and other events can change a person's perception of himself in areas that are peripheral to core beliefs.

d) **The self-concept has a dimension which evaluates its perceptions, the self-esteem.** The evaluations that are held about core perceptions are also less resistant to change than are evaluations about perceptions which are not as central to the core. Peripheral evaluations are more likely to be

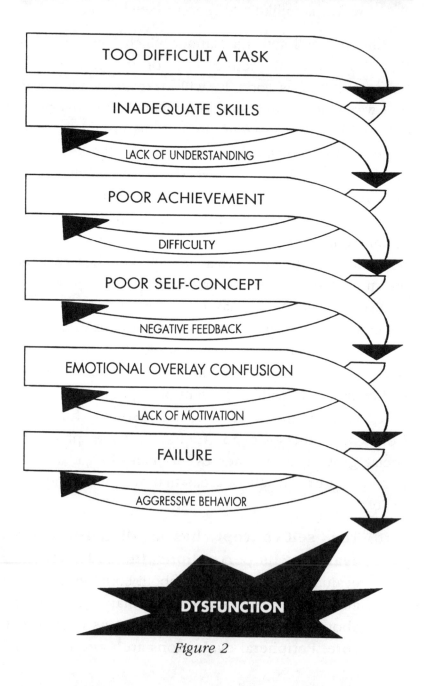

Figure 2

modified because of the strength of their importance to the individual. One's perception of oneself as a skier or as a cook is usually not as central to one's core beliefs as a child and consequently has received less reinforcement to establish the belief. Consequently, changes in less firmly fixed perceptions are more likely to occur.

Largely because the self-concept has a tendency for consistency, children with negative beliefs about themselves are unlikely to believe evidence to the contrary. When praise or approval is given in areas for which the child holds a negative belief, he will reject the praise. When children have negative self-esteem, their behavior reflects this belief.

The analogy of training the elephant referred to in the introduction of this book is a case in point. And so it is with people. Irrespective of the truth of the situation in which we may find ourselves, we respond to the situation based on the belief structure of our abilities or our inabilities. The image that we hold of ourselves controls our behavior.

The good news is that we can change. We are not stuck with who we are. Through techniques explored in the remainder of this book, you will learn how to modify the belief system (figure 2) and consequently effect positive change in personal behavior.

SUMMARY OF CHAPTER TWO

1. Self-esteem is one of the most important factors influencing success at school.

2. The self-concept:

   a) is multidimensional

   b) is hierarchical

   c) reasonably stable and consistent

   d) has a dimension which evaluates its perceptions, the self-esteem

3 Research Findings

The proof of any program is found in its performance. Investigations of programs claiming to have a positive impact on students reveal that few have been empirically tested. The logic inherent in a planned program often does not materialize when implemented. The strategies recommended in this text have been implemented in a variety of settings and with age groups varying from 10 to 55 years. It has been used in sport and academic settings, with teachers, students and adults.

The data reported here was collected based on over 100 secondary school students ranging in ages from 16 to 19. They were part of a marriage and family relations class and volunteered to take part in the program. Many of the students were initially skeptical of the potential effects of the program. However, following an explanation of the program, all committed themselves to making an honest effort to comply with the recommended procedures. Commitment is personally important to the students. It is this quality that distinguished the benefits of this program from *just another course* taken at school. The fact that the benefits of this program can have a profound personal bearing outside of school easily persuaded students that this course is somehow unique. Once committment was obtained, the program began.

The Program

The program consists of eight stages. These include:

1. Relaxation Any exercise or activity that the teacher feels is appropriate for the class may be used. (See Chapter 6)

2. Becoming aware of negative attitudes and internal dialogue and development of a counter-acting positive statement. (See Chapter 7)

3. Self-esteem list. Making a list of positive qualities the person already possesses. (See Chapter 3)

4. Seeking positive experiences. These experiences must be achievable. (See Chapter 8)

5. Developing a Winning Feeling. The individuals must learn to get themselves into the same state they were in when they performed at their best in the past. With practice they will be able to move into this state at will. (See Chapter 8)

6. List of personal affirmative statements. This is a list of skills or personality traits that the students would like to work toward. (See Chapter 8)

7. Develop an image of the type of person they would like to become. (See Chapter 8)

8. Visualize. Students learn to visualize the performance perfectly. At this stage they take all of the qualities they would like to perform and put them all together. (See Chapter 7 and 8).

Program Implementation

That was a brief summary of the program that was administered to the students in this sample. What follows is a typical presentation and explanation of the experiences provided to aid in the implementation of the course in another setting.

The relaxation component of the program is usually well received by everyone. A taped program that asks the students to do a series of muscle relaxation exercises is followed by a series of mental exercises. Students often find this stage exciting because they think they have been hypnotized. Most people have never intentionally caused themselves to enter a deep relaxation state. When students quickly discover their ability to enter this state at will, the uplifting sensation is very pleasurable. Any activity that aids students to enter the relaxed state of mind is useful (see Chapter 6). The teacher will have to *read the class* to determine the best procedure to use.

The goal of this section is to have the students become aware of the sensation of being relaxed. This is followed by repeated practice to be able to bring about this feeling at will.

It is also important to make students aware of tension that may be in their body at any time. Learning to identify these areas leads to more understanding of themselves and their reactions to stress. The more control students develop, the greater their potential to enter a relaxed and productive state of mind. Many students choose to lie on the floor when relaxing. Some will fall asleep. Obviously this can be problematic in terms of being able to proceed with the rest of the program (but it does reduce discipline problems). The association of relaxation exercises to sleep can be counter-productive. The desired state is one of mentally focused relaxation. It is important to stress that the purpose of the exercise is to enter a state in which to be able to function at a higher mental level. Sleep is not such a state!

Once the relaxation state can be brought about with ease, students are ready for the next step. This is to have the students develop an awareness of the attitudes they hold toward themselves, to be able to articulate their self-concept. At this stage, the student is becoming aware of the self-talk, both positive and negative, that goes on in his mind. Most people have little difficulty noting what others have said about them and in turn, what they think and say about themselves. Once they are aware of what they are saying to themselves, they need to summarize these statements into two or three simple thoughts. It is sometimes difficult to find positive statements to counteract the debilitating effects of the negative attitudes that many students harbor. Usually students will present several statements that they hear themselves say repeatedly.

The challenge for the teacher at this point is to work with the students to help them summarize their list into two or three statements. Once this is done, a positive statement must be written that the student can substitute for the negative. This can be time consuming, often using as much as two hours of class time to complete the task. One hurdle that may have to be overcome occurs when a student lists a negative statement like, "I'm lazy," and now must come up with a positive counteracting statement. The counteracting statement that a student writes is often phrased like "I will not be so lazy." Writing a statement in this fashion is ineffective for a couple of reasons.

Positive statements, or affirmations, have three qualities that are essential for effective implementation. First, they must be written in the first person singular using the pronoun "I." Second, positive statements must be written in the present tense. And finally, affirmations must be written in positive terminology stating what is to occur, not stating what is not to occur. The mind cannot focus on the inverse of an idea. So stating "I will not be so lazy," is ineffective because it is written negatively in the future tense indicating what will be avoided and not what will be done. The term *lazy* might be better substituted as follows. "I am hard working and energetic." Other statements that are more goal oriented might be, "I enjoy doing homework before I watch TV at night." Having students write statements in their own language following these guidelines is often more effective than a statement written by the teacher. The process for change is now ready to begin. In a relaxed state, students can now chant, sing, recite or use any other method that will start to change their internal dialogue.

The next section of the program involves the students making a list of their positive personal qualities. This stage is called "developing a self-esteem list." The students are instructed to develop a list of personal qualities in which they believe they have some strength. Some students experience difficulty with this task. Many believe that their positive qualities are of little value stating "Everyone has that ability," or because of upbringing that rewards modesty, are reluctant to publicly state "Here's what I'm good at." Teachers have effectively used the strategy of telling students that even though their quality may be shared by others, that it is still desirable and can be considered to be a strength. This too, can be a time consuming activity but one that is very worthwhile and ultimately beneficial for immediate enhancement of a student's self-feelings.

A good starting point for this activity is with popular music. Having a love of music is a positive quality. Another easily identifiable characteristic is the ability to understand popular movies. The ability to remember plots or the words to songs is another common ability. These skills are shared by many students and can be seen as personal strengths and a good place to begin this activity for those who may experience difficulty with the task.

Once the pattern begins, it often continues into other areas. The self-esteem list used in Herbert Otto's book, *More Joy In Your Marriage,* is particularly useful. There are many other lists available in positive health books that can be very effective. Another successful method is to brainstorm positive characteristics that individuals may possess. This can help students when their list is compared with the lists provided by the *experts* as the lists will be very similar.

The focus in the program to this point has been on students gathering information about themselves to heighten their personal awareness of themselves. What follows is designed to create personal behavioral changes so that the students can begin to develop a new history about themselves. The emphasis is on achievable activities leading to positive accomplishment. Success must be assured!

For some students, arriving on time to class once during a week may be a measurable improvement over current behavior. Together, the student and teacher meet to determine an appropriate first goal (See Chapter 5). Developing a foundation of accomplishment may take several months. The teacher is often the motivating force to keep the program alive and the students on task and focused. With many students potentially working on different goals, it is essential for both the motivation of the student and the teacher's organization that the individual goals be documented. Because of the important role of the teacher to the success of this program, keeping the goal of *developing the student's potential to the highest* must be central in the teacher's mind at all times.

Because of provincial and state mandates to cover prescribed amounts of curriculum per term, teachers often feel forced to *plow on* teaching subject matter at the expense of the student's personal development. This is a critical issue in education, especially at the secondary level, but not one without acceptable alternative approaches that foster human development.

Developing a *winning feeling* is the next stage in the program. This stage can be one of the most exciting parts of the program because the teacher encourages the student to remember feelings of excitement and well-being, times when everything in the student's life was going well. Most students are able to remember something that felt extremely positive as they did it. They also find it easy to remember and re-experience the feelings they had when they were on a personal high. Occasionally, some students are unable to recall such an personal experience. Encouraging them to imagine the feeling of accomplishing something worthwhile, or reliving an especially moving scene from a positive movie can have similar effects. If the teacher feels comfortable, he can relate to the class as an example a moving experience to allow the class to imagine the feeling that such an event might have. The more hype that can be made of this section, the better. The more positive emotions that can be recalled the better. See Chapter 8 on the Winning Feeling for more details on this procedure.

Developing a list of personal affirmative statements involves working toward a new belief system. In this next section, the focus is on working toward the type of person that the student would like to be. The teacher will ask the student to act-as-if and suspend honesty and belief. "What kind of person would you like to be?" or "How would you rather act differently than you are now?" or, "Ten years from now, how would you like to be?" Any phrasing such as the above will start the students thinking about the way they would like to behave. This stage of the program involves thinking of the future and using the goal-setting chapters to make some progress in this regard. Many students find this hard to do, possibly because they lack the imagination to see themselves in a positive future. Their present experience gives them little to choose from and little background to base positive visualizations upon. If difficulties arise in this area, having students identify with their heroes, be they from TV, the movies, books or real life people, can aid in beginning this process. Having the students think about this future in a variety of areas, such as personal life, career, recreational activities, hobbies, personality styles, lifestyle, marital status, etc., can also be an effective starting point. If difficulties still persist, photos from magazines may help to trigger students to think about their future. One effective technique is to try to have students identify with a hero or heroine who will become their model for future behavior.

Once established, the students can move on to the next stage which is to develop an image of the type of person they would like to be. They must now begin to identify those qualities and characteristics they would like to work toward. If a list is needed to assist, the teacher and student can make one together. Some students do not need to make lists because they can visualize exactly how they would like to behave based on the role model they have identified. The clearer the futuristic image is, the more powerful the effects of the exercise.

In the final stage, students are taught to visualize the type of person they would like to become as clearly as possible. They are asked to see themselves in the position behaving perfectly. They are to imagine themselves behaving in all activities from beginning to end using all the senses where possible. Students are instructed to enter a relaxed and alert mode. They are then to visualize all the qualities of the person that they would like to be. By processing this image, students are constructing new neural pathways and allowing their belief system to begin to overtake the old way of thinking with the new. Once they can see themselves performing well in the new area, they are taught to anchor their winning feelings with the new way of behaving. By trying to make this process as exciting as possible, fuel in the form of emotional energy is added to the process.

In a nutshell, this is the program proposed in this text. Experience from teachers who have administered the program indicates that the most demanding aspect is for the teacher to keep the momentum for change going and to keep the students focused on their goals. An effective way to begin is for teachers to go through the process first themselves. In this way, teachers will have first hand experience at the process the students will be involved with. This greatly adds credibility in the eyes of the students to the teacher's position as an instructor.

Many teachers have visualized themselves teaching the program to a group of students. They have imagined themselves successfully presenting the material to the class. They have seen the students enthusiastically buying into the ideas presented. And they have seen themselves modifying the program and making the necessary personal adjustments to meet the individual student's needs. Such visualizing has been the source of confidence to many teachers beginning to work with new material.

Research Findings

As stated earlier, the proof of any program is in its effectiveness to cause desired change. When this program was initially implemented with secondary schools students, the areas of interest in terms of behavioral change were academic achievement, attendance, interpersonal relations and more generally, how students felt about themselves.

What began as a mini-program lasting two periods has grown over three years to become an integral part of the guidance program. The course is in heavy demand from students and is fully supported by staff for the positive results that are evident. The response to the program has been outstanding. Adult groups have commented, "Why couldn't we have had a program like this when we were in high school?" At the outset, the goal of the program was to increase awareness of self-esteem and the possibilities for enhancing it.

Far more than the initial goals have been realized! Of over 125 students, only four said that they were influenced little by the program. When these students were investigated further, it was found that events in their lives were so overbearing that only intense individual help would have been effective.

Findings

It is important to keep in mind as you read these findings that the students involved in the program have been identified as at risk in academic, social or family environments. The sample is not randomly selected, but specially selected because of identified personal needs.

Attendance: 46 percent reported improved attendance at school. Keep in mind, however, that not all students were in need of improving their attendance at classes.

Skipping classes: 90 percent reported less skipping of classes.

Lateness: 60 percent reported being late for class less frequently.

Grade improvement: 57 percent reported better averages. Marked improvement ranged from 2 to 20 percent.

Relationships: with friends   85 percent improvement

with parents   73 percent improvement

with teachers   81 percent improvement

with classmates 91 percent improvement

with siblings   82 percent improvement

The Future: 95 percent reported feeling optimistic about their future.

Control of the Future: 83 percent reported they felt in control of their life in the future.

Program effectiveness: In response to the question, "Has the program helped you in any way?" Ninety percent reported that the program had personally helped them and that they had recommended it to others.

Outlook on life: 90 percent reported an improvement.

Achievement: 81 percent of the students reported that their work habits had improved and that they were working more efficiently and working more diligently on their goals.

Confidence in self: 88 percent reported being more confident about themselves.

Recognizing that with the exception of academic grades, attendance, skipping and reported lates for class, the results are self-reported perceptions. Personal perception however is a key quality to behavioral change. The fact that the student's sense of empowerment has dramatically increased is what is key to assessing the effectiveness of this program.

The overall feeling of students, instructors and other academic staff that surrounds this program is that it does positively effect the students and is an agent for real change in their lives. Educationally, the students were more excited about coming to class and performing better. They generally felt that relationships with everyone had improved and that they had more control of where they were going.

4   The Change Process

Many people in all walks of life accept the idea that they cannot be successful. It becomes a way of life for them. They choose careers, houses, holidays, lifestyles and even husbands and wives that are below what they are capable of or worthy of achieving. The Belief System sets up what is believed to be true. Brain patterns which form in the mind process all our perceptions and experiences in terms of those beliefs. Many potentially talented people choose situations in their lives below the level of which they are capable because their Belief System will not allow them to go after a dream. In one situation, a student who had maintained a 4.0 average over four years in high school was interested in law as a career. Guidance counselors tried unsuccessfully to convince her of her ability to succeed at law school. Instead, she chose to become a legal secretary. Being a lawyer in her eyes was just *out of her league*. The Belief System had claimed another one! Another student dreamed of a career in show business. In a counselling office he began to cry. Everything he ever wanted never came true! And he did not expect that this dream would be any different! Chalk up one more for the Belief System. In both of these cases, it was the Belief System that set the limits on the levels of performance, not the person's ability. People accepted a life and personal performance below that which they were capable. There is an old adage which is so very true, "It is not what you are that holds you back, it's what you think you are not!" The ingrained Belief System...what a powerful force!

Our beliefs are based on what all of our life's experiences have taught us about ourselves. We are governed by the attitudes and expectations we hold about ourselves. For us, these attitudes and expectations become the mind structure by which all our experiences are assessed to determine if they are in line with the real world. We believe these things so strongly that we will rationalize experiences that are contrary to our beliefs in order to maintain inner consistency. Reality then becomes what we believe to be true, not what really is. Consequently, we respond to our perception of the world as reality. And our perceptions are filtered through our Belief System.

Isn't it interesting how we perceive someone we love? As adolescents we feel the person we are dating is just about perfect. When the romance cools, we often ask ourselves, "what did I ever see in them?" Initially, we thought they were perfect. Later, we saw so many negative qualities, the romance ended. The behavior of the person in question has likely remained consistent. What changed was our perception of that person. There are many other examples. Consider a job we thought was terrific at one point and at another we wanted out of it so badly we quit. The job didn't change. What had changed was our perception of the experience. Consider, too, a family event. In speaking to other family members after the event it is often interesting to note how differently the same experience may have been perceived by those people involved. The same event may have different meanings for each family member. It is perception that determines our reality! And the world we perceive is filtered by our Belief System.

Because of the importance of the Belief System it is essential to examine some of the major influences that affect it. We know that the Belief System becomes programmed by events in our life. This programming makes connections within our brain which become the major way we will process any event we consciously perceive. Patterns of neural activity develop so that information is processed in the same way time and time again. Any new event is assessed with this patterned response. If there is inconsistency between our experience of an event and our Belief System we rationalize the perception to maintain inner consistency with our beliefs. However if an experience can be perceived to be in line with our beliefs, the information is used to reinforce what we already believe to be true. As more evidence is gathered, one can confidently say "life is really the way I know it...everyone else must be wrong because I know I am right."

For instance, when teaching students, we can give examples of our programmed selves. We can ask our students to reflect and think about a time when they did something their parents viewed as unacceptable. It may have been cheating on an exam, drinking alcohol, using drugs, becoming involved with sex or breaking a curfew. Although the activity may have been enjoyable, deep inside they were aware that what they were doing was unacceptable. Anxiety sets in. This feeling can usually not be resolved until an adjustment is made to the Belief System or the behavior is altered to allow a feeling of comfort to return.

Our self-concept regulates our behavior by assessing it. This is an emotional response...either negative or positive. Regardless of which it is, signals are sent back into our subconscious which eventually affects our level of self-esteem. This process is repeated many times a day to confirm our Belief System.

In the course of our development, we are influenced by a variety of experiences. Think about the experience of going to school. Most students begin with the idea that school will be an exciting place to be. In the latter years of high school, behavior ranges in extreme from dedication to studies at one end, to classes being skipped and open defiance of the system at the other. Schools are an interesting influence. Some educators, whether by choice or chance, create an environment in which their students feel good about themselves so that they can make mistakes, adjust, and learn. Other educators have the opposite influence and turn students off. In general, schools tend to put students down. Many students feel that schools play a game called *take-away*. If an answer is inadequate, the student perception is that marks will be taken away from one's grade. Increasingly, students develop behavior and expectations that place them in a *hope I pass* mode.

Music, too, has an influence upon us. Subtle and not so subtle messages are driven into our conscious and subconscious minds influencing life-styles and beliefs. People listen to music which is usually in line with what they believe. Research has demonstrated the powerful impact of words on attitudes and beliefs. The effect of a new rock star or style of music can be easily seen in the styles of clothing, use of language, behavior and attitudes. In North America, rap music, with its catchy words is now trying to influence young people to avoid using drugs.

The influence of parents and home life can also be very dramatic. The Mormon Church is most aware of the power of the family on developing youth. They actively advertise their message in commercials to support and influence families toward positive personal interactions. Friends too are a powerful influence. They are constantly there reinforcing beliefs. Peer pressure to conform with the beliefs of the group are, to parents and teachers, disturbingly powerful forces. It's quite easy to watch behavior change as new friends are developed. A choice between conforming to group norms or leaving the group is often the only option seemingly open to youth. Both options may be seen to have negative consequences to a youth who must make a difficult decision.

There is no question that schools, church, home, friends, music, religion and parents influence Belief Systems and ultimately attitudes, expectations and behavior. Some experiences influence us more than others because some events are more emotionally significant than others. Significant emotional events become mental landmarks that influence the way the world is perceived. The greater the emotions attached to any experience, the greater the impact. Reflect back to your own teen years. Think about a first love; being chosen last for teams; being put down by someone you really cared about; or being rejected by someone. Conversely, think about how wonderful it was to win; solve a problem; or how beautiful it was to be loved by someone. We've all had experiences like these. Attached to these experiences are feelings of the event, be they positive or negative.

Our attitude toward events and experiences determine the direction we will take and the decisions we will make in our life. A common belief is that to make changes in one's Belief System involves a major revision. There may be some truth in this. Frequently however, a minor adjustment may lead to a major change in one's life. People tend to become comfortable in their way of life even though they may wish for a better quality of life or better performance from themselves. While feeling comfortable, they will at the same time make excuses for not performing better. Excuses like,

"Someday I'll...," or "when I finally get this done then...," or "I'm just not like that...," etc., etc. The subconscious mind tends to direct individuals to perform in ways that will confirm beliefs held to be true about themselves. A lack of success is often not situational. A lack of success is often caused by one's Belief System that allows or disallows concrete actions to improve one's performance to be taken. Maxwell Maltz stated that the mind is a guidance mechanism. It functions by processing events to be seen consistently in terms of what one believes to be true about oneself. When one functions or behaves outside the subconscious reality, an uneasiness will result signaling a need to return to the *normal* levels of behavior. The mind has been programmed to behave within the reality the Belief System has generated. Once established, attitudes and expectations about virtually everything experienced will be colored by this outlook. In order to cause real change, attitudes about oneself have to be changed...a reprogramming of the mind is required!

All of us have been moved by an inspirational speaker or a significant emotional event. Immediately following this, behavior often changes, but usually only for a short period of time. The key to successful long term change is a reprogramming of the Belief System. To offer incentives to a person to cause change requires that an unlimited supply of incentives or rewards be available. For the most part, this is impractical and unworkable in the long term. This approach either becomes cost prohibitive or the initial impact of the incentive becomes diminished in its effect. To really cause change, an individual has to internalize a new set of attitudes or perceptions about oneself. Simply addressing the fact that a change is needed can be very negative because it focuses on the problem, on the negative. What is needed is a more positive approach, a more proactive versus reactive approach.

We have seen now that beliefs create attitudes. Attitudes create feelings about ourselves. And it is feelings that determine actions. Through actions, results occur. But let's not get ahead of ourselves. For just a moment, let's backtrack a bit. Before improved performance can happen, new attitudes and beliefs about life have to be developed. In some situations this may require a major overhaul in attitude. In many cases however, only a slight revision may be all that is needed. Generally, most people operate relatively efficiently. A little fine tuning of the system may cause enough of a change in attitude to modify behavior to reach new levels of success. This idea is really important in order for change to occur. It must be accepted that change can and need occur. As noted earlier, behavior is rooted in belief about what can or cannot be done. All our personal information is stored subconsciously as a functioning reality filter. This filter assesses every piece of information and accepts or rejects it in agreement with the individual's Belief System. This is a continuous process that functions as we perceive our world.

Change motivation can come from a variety of sources and circumstances. One fact, however, is certain. Some significant emotional event, some triggering device must occur that effects core components making up the Belief System which will provide the motivation for the development of human potential. Most people believe that they have something worthwhile to contribute to our society. Many people are frustrated at their seeming lack of ability to attain this potential.

The emotional event can occur incidentally, or individuals can take a proactive stance and effect a change in a systematic way on their own. It is the latter approach that will be investigated throughout the remainder of this book.

SUMMARY CHAPTER FOUR

1. We develop a Belief System which creates our reality. All of our perceptions of the world are filtered through our Belief System. We respond to those filtered perceptions as if they were true, irrespective of what the truth of a situation might be.

2. The Belief System influences the attitudes, expectations that we have and behavior which we exhibit.

5 Goal Setting as a Tool for Empowerment

"Cheshire-Puss," she began rather timidly...
"Would you tell me, please, which way I ought to go
from here."
"That depends a good deal on where you want to get to,"
said the cat.
"I don't much care where...," said Alice.
"Then it doesn't matter which way you go," said the cat.
-- *Lewis Carroll, Alice in Wonderland*

To choose a direction, to choose a path! It really doesn't matter much what we decide, if we don't have an idea on where we want to go, our chances of being successful in a manner that is personally rewarding are greatly minimized.

Jack Donohue, formerly Canada's Olympic and National basketball coach, tells a story about Susan Nattrass, six-time world champion in trap shooting. He claimed that he could beat her easily in shooting, with one small advantage. She had to be blindfolded. That's ridiculous, some said. How can she hit a target she can't see? That was precisely his point. You can't hit a target you can't see!

We all require a target in which to direct our energies and our efforts. Can you imagine how popular the game of bowling would be if a blanket were to be placed in front of the pins. What fun would there be if you didn't know what you were aiming at? How satisfying would it be if you could only hear the pins falling, but had no idea which ones fell?

Where do you direct the next ball?

This may be a simplistic analogy, but the psychological components involved in bowling are not too far removed from the psychological factors at play in school and in the work place. We need to know where we are going and what we still require to do to be successful.

Few teachers have a specific plan for improving their own psychological readiness for the event of teaching. Even fewer students have goals that are personalized, realistic and relevant to their level of development. How to set goals and pursue them is not normally part of the educational experience of most students. Yet this is so essential for us all. Specific preparation and performance goals can be of incredible benefit to teachers and students alike.

When one experiences an accomplishment obtained through personal perseverance and determined effort, a feeling of satisfaction is strongly felt. When one experiences moments of success, one feels in control and personally responsible for the direction in which life is progressing. A sense of empowerment develops. This is an essential quality for all people to experience if a positive sense of self-esteem is to be realized.

Historically, schools have focused the energy devoted to curriculum development on the content areas and the acquisition of knowledge. For many years, researchers have been aware of the skills and strategies available to use with students to improve the psychological climate within a school. However, teachers, being as overworked as they are, have often viewed such suggestions as just one more thing to add to an already burdensome workload. Teachers have often regarded innovations as frills to do either instead of, or in addition to, the existing program of study that is mandated to be covered.

As educators, we are very much aware that there are many individual students who are experiencing problems which can be traced to low self-esteem. Increasing crime rates, increased abuse of drugs and alcohol, discouraging dropout rates and chronic behavior problems are but a few of the signs that something is amiss with our young. Nearly 20 years ago, in the early 1970's, researchers discovered that the longer students stayed in school, as a group, the lower their self-esteem scores became. This information is not new to professionals in education. Yet despite this knowledge, little has been done that has been successful in addressing this phenomena.

Students of course, have no control over the level of academic ability with which they are born. Nonetheless, Bloom (1981) writes that 90 to 95 percent of students are endowed with ample ability to successfully deal with the content objectives of the school curriculum. In order to work at this level, there are three conditions, which must be met. One, students have enough time on task; two, students can work in optimum learning environments; and three, students are willing to invest appropriate levels of effort to the task.

Time on task and creating an appropriate learning environment are traditionally seen as being in the control of teachers. Dedicating an appropriate level of effort has been usually viewed as solely within the control of the student. While there may be some truth to this perception, teachers can intervene to control some factors within the learning environment that can be instrumental in increasing the rate of success and accomplishment that each student experiences. When the incidence of accomplishment increases, the intrinsic motivation of the student will correspondingly increase.

Brophy (1984, 1986) has developed a theory of student motivation. In this theory, Brophy believes that an equation of

EFFORT = EXPECTANCY X VALUE describes student motivation. In this model, the amount of effort that can be expected from students is a product of two things: the expectations that the student has for being successful on the task; and two, the value that the student places on completing the task.

Many programs that are currently in place in public education are aimed at providing greater challenges and rewards to the upper 50 percentile. This focus will probably result in greater effort and production from this group. At the same time, academic competition will also likely increase producing an even greater threat to the academic self-esteem of less able students. A defense mechanism for these students is to become apathetic. If one holds back and does not try, one can always rationalize and personally save face by saying, "I really could do it if I tried."

A good analogy can be found in the story of the tortoise and the hare. Such a race benefits neither participant. The hare becomes lazy and sluggish while the tortoise can become discouraged at the slim prospect of winning. What is required is a technique, a race if you will to continue the analogy, that will be to the benefit of both runners. Individualized goal setting is one tool that can be just that.

This chapter will explore goal setting as a successful strategy to enhance student self-esteem and to invite apathetic students to become personally committed to the learning process. This is exciting! And it works! Let's see how.

The Goal Setting Model

May 6, 1954 is a day that will go down in sport history as one of the most memorable. For years preceding this day, literally thousands of competitors had been attempting to break the four minute mile. Since the days of the early

Greeks, this had been a barrier that had withheld the best attempts of man. But no matter how people tried, no one was able to break this mark. So, people believed it to be impossible. This belief was supported by very logical reasons ...wind resistance was too great...inadequate lung capacity... the human bone structure was inappropriate...physiologically it was just impossible! The reasons were numerous and varied.

Then on May 6, Roger Bannister proved that all the experts and the thousands of people who had tried and failed before him were all wrong. Bannister believed in himself...not in the experts! Within the next 12 months following the shattering of this milestone, 37 other runners had broken the four minute barrier. By 1956, over 300 runners had broken the four minute mile.

The significant difference in the world of athletics was not in training techniques, equipment or the human bone structure. What did change was personal attitudes on the part of the athletes. Now, for the first time, people believed that they could break the four minute mile and went out and acted as if it was possible, and it was!

Goals can be accomplished...if they are set! It doesn't matter if others claim that you are not as smart, or as hardworking, or as competent as other people. What does matter ultimately is what you say about yourself.

Goal setting is a means of making those dreams come true. Goals are dreams on a time line!

Goal Setting with Kids: Some Considerations

Children have many needs that go beyond the school curriculum. Too often in pursuit of the mandate given to teachers, the focus becomes the teaching of the curriculum instead of the teaching of the child. This has almost become a cliche in educational circles, but it is nonetheless true. When setting objectives with children, keep the total child in focus considering social, emotional, behavioral, physical and intellectual needs.

To Begin

- When introducing students to goal setting, it is important that the teacher encourages students to set goals that are: 1) short term and 2) easily attainable. This will ensure that the student realizes success quickly and will begin to feel good about the goal setting program.

- The goals should be based on the knowledge that the student and the teacher share about the student's past abilities, accomplishments and experiences. This greatly assists in establishing goals that are personally relevant to an individual.

- Goals can be established that can have varying time lines. For some students, a goal might be to sit quietly for five minutes. For another, a goal might be to be more actively involved in class discussions. This might take the form of volunteering to answer two questions during a thirty minute class.

Other goals may be set to be operating for a day, a week, a term or the whole school year. Because of the individualized nature of a goal setting program, a teacher and student must jointly assess where a student is currently functioning and then plan a course of action that will direct the student's efforts toward the desired goal.

With Children

- *Goals need to have direction which implies specificity.* A distinction needs to be made between wishes, wants and goals. Often children wish that things would happen and they would be happy if they happened. However in the case of wishes, a student is not willing to make a commitment and to provide the effort needed to improve the chances that the wish will come true. Similarly, a want is something that a student would like to have occur. The student is also willing to make a commitment to do what is required to increase the probability that success will occur. Both wishes and wants refer to general performance outcomes that any individual would like to have happen. However, they are not goals!

- *Goals must be specific!* They must be written in behavioral terms based on the student's past personal performance, characteristics and qualities related to a given area. The goal must be written as precisely as possible so that there is no doubt in the student's mind about what needs to be done. For instance, to allow a student to have as a goal "happiness" is too general and lacks direction. Alternatively, determining what makes an individual happy and then trying to do more of these activities is behaviorally written and is more appropriate as a goal. This approach provides direction for the student.

- *Self-controlled.* Goals for children need to be written in behavioral terms over which the child has control. Goals should not be written in terms that deal with behaviors or performances that depend upon other people.

- *Measurable*. Ideally, goals should be written in such a way so that the desired behavior can be measured objectively. This is not always possible, however, so a subjective assessment may need to be agreed upon. What is crucial is that there is some means of determining student progress toward the desired goal.

  For instance, if we know that a student is able to run comfortably for six minutes, it might be reasonable to ask that student on the next outing attempt to run for perhaps seven minutes. This is measurable and is based on the student's past level of performance. This approach builds a level of accomplishment which increasingly acts as a foundation of comfort for the student when trying to reach loftier goals.

- *Challenging*. A goal must provide a challenge for a student. The goal ideally will be set sufficiently beyond the present level of the student's capability to force him to extend himself. Setting goals in such a manner will require the student to exert effort and persistence to reach the new level of performance.

  When this situation occurs, and students are successful in their attempts, a feeling of satisfaction accompanies the reaching of the goal. If the goal is too easy, the outcome of the assigned task is known from the outset and no sense of satisfaction is attained, only relief that yet another assignment is completed. If the goal is too difficult, the outcome is frustration and frequently this is also known from the outset. Only when the outcome is unknown, when the goal is located in that deliciously uncertain area of performance is satisfaction and the feeling of success attained.

- *Achievable*. While a goal must be challenging, at the same time it must be be set at a level that the possibilities of success are very real. This is not to suggest that success should come on every attempt. This would be a case of too low a level of challenge. By achievable, it is implied that the goal is set just out of the grasp of where the student is currently functioning. With suitable effort and persistence, the goal can be attained. This assumes that the teacher knows where the student is currently functioning so that realistic and achievable goals can be set.

- *Time Line*. A goal must be set with a specific time frame for completion. Setting a time line adds to the motivational impact for the student. The time line that is set must be a factor when one determines the achievability of the goal. Obviously, the more demanding a goal, the longer the time allowed to complete it can be. Similarly, the level of difficulty associated with a goal can be a function of the time line assigned to it. For instance, a goal that could be viewed as very attainable in a one week time frame, could be seen as being very difficult if only two days are permitted.

- *Dynamic*. Goals and the progress that is being made in pursuit of them needs to be under continual supervision. This is especially true when a teacher is getting to know a student and when students are new to setting goals. If it is seen that a goal is too difficult, this should be discussed and more realistic goals set in their place. The same is true for goals that are obviously so easy so as not to be challenging.

For Success

- *Goals must be personalized.* For students to have a feeling of being successful, they must work toward something that has personal meaning to them. Obviously we cannot allow a child to develop his own course of study. That is not what is implied. However, in conjunction with the teacher, students should be directed as to what needs to be done. Then the student should be allowed input as to what will be done and the manner and time line to complete the task.

Goals should also be set, not only in areas of personal weakness, but in areas where a student has strength as well. It is critical that students have the opportunity to frequently experience strong positive emotions attached to areas of success so that the sense of empowerment can continue to develop. Focusing on areas of weakness only in a goal setting program will convey the message to the student that hidden under this approach to learning is a considerable amount of work and frustration. This is not significantly better than what students are currently experiencing.

The development of a goal setting program is the combined effort and knowledge of a teacher and a student.

One way of looking at goal setting is that it is a long-term means of keeping track of your time. What is involved with this approach is:

- setting goals
- developing a strategy to attain the goals
- follow through with the plan

What follows is a seven step model that has been used successfully with students in elementary and secondary schools. The seven steps are:

1. committing the goal to writing
2. understanding the goal
3. developing a plan to attain the goals
4. identifying problems in attaining the goals
5. strategies for dealing with the problems
6. setting a time line for implementation
7. review/reassess the goals

Step 1: Committing the Goal to Writing

To begin, it needs to be clearly understood that for goals to be meaningful to students, they need to be theirs. That is, the students need to come to a decision about what their needs are and what needs to be accomplished. This decision can be made with the assistance of the teacher, but the final decision needs to be made by the student. When students are free to decide on their own goals and their own course of action, their level of aspiration tends to function as a protective mechanism. Protection is built in by the student in two important ways. First, students will set goals to avoid repeated failure from objectives that are too difficult, and secondly, they will protect themselves against goals that are too easy and do not give a feeling of success. This is the ideal! Teachers who know their students can act as a guide in the early stages to assist students in this regard.

Often teachers assign work for students to complete with a due date. The assignment has been preplanned to fit into the overall objectives of a unit of study. However, one of the obstacles teachers face daily, is following up on student work that has gone undone. Part of the reason for the lack of student follow through is that the work that has been assigned does not address student needs, interests or the developmental level at which the student is currently operating.

For anyone to have the persistence to follow through in the pursuit of a goal, there must be personal ownership in the goal.

Once the decision about what the goal is...write it down. One requires a clear idea about the nature of a goal in order to be able to commit the idea to paper. To write down a goal, it must be clear and definite in one's mind. The act of writing goals down forces one to think more clearly about what is to be accomplished.

So often in school, students simply *roll along* and take part without ever carefully considering what their priorities in an activity are, or how to realize them. Alan Lakein (1973), one of the foremost writers of time management, writes that goal setting is the first step to *getting control of your time and your life.*

Even young students can benefit immensely from the clarification that goal setting provides. For example, being aware that, in order to attain a higher grade in the social sciences, certain criteria needs to be met will greatly increase the motivation to addressing this requirement. There are important research skills, note-keeping skills, and participation and knowledge requirements that all contribute to the final grade that a student can receive. This knowledge can contribute to the creation of numerous meaningful sub-goals that all contribute to attaining the main goal.

Writing down the main and sub-goals is the first step in being able to conceptualize what is required on the part of the student. The goal becomes more than *I want to do well*, or *I want to get better grades.* Now, often for the first time, students can see what needs to be done in concrete terms.

Items written down such as, attending class daily, completing daily assignments, asking at least one question in class daily, and keeping a homework book up to date are personal goals that allow a student to see what is necessary for success.

Step Two: Understanding the Goal

Talk About it With Others

Before students can begin to realistically address the question of how to accomplish a goal, they need to fully understand what the goal is all about. For instance, many students may wish to become faster in reciting math facts. However, they may fail to realize that speed in recall often requires many hours of practice over a number of weeks, time that is often done at home with parents in addition to the practice provided at school. This is an implication for the student to realize before agreeing to pursue this particular type of goal.

Having the opportunity to talk about these implications with the teacher and to perhaps obtain a set of flash cards or drill sheets for home use sets the ground work for the student to begin working toward the goal.

With Children

As previously mentioned, students need the opportunity to talk about what it is they are trying to accomplish so that they have a clear mental picture of where they are going. Teachers need to assume the role of facilitators. In this role, staff members can help students to imagine themselves being successful in obtaining the goal. This may mean drawing pictures of the goal for young children, or mentally seeing themselves as successful in achieving the goal for older students.

When a teacher shows confidence in a student by working together on a plan that involves assessment, program planning and goal setting strategies, the likelihood that students will feel comfortable in talking to the teacher about their concerns or suggestions increases also. Teachers are there to encourage students to pursue their own goals. To be the best that they can be! That is the primary objective behind personal goal setting.

For Success

As facilitators, teachers can aid students in confirming their committment to the goal. Students need to continue to confirm the goal in their own mind, and to continue dialoguing with the teacher so that the desire to work toward the goal remains strong. Many teachers have noticed declining desire in students to follow through. They have also noticed that the goal was either too long term in its design, or that the reward (either intrinsic or extrinsic) was not meaningful to the student. These are two areas that may need to be addressed when lack of desire is evident.

Step Three: Plan the Journey

Plan the Goal in Stages

In order to begin any trip, one needs to know where the starting point is. For many students, they are not aware of what they know and what they don't know. This is where the teachers assistance is invaluable. The teacher should be aware of the students strengths and weaknesses in relation to the set goal. Staff members can recommend to students where they should begin on their journey.

In the early stages of a goal setting program, it is a good idea to allow a student to work at a slightly easier level in pursuit of the goal so that success is assured without too much frustration.

A long term goal, once established, needs to be accompanied by a series of progressive short term goals that lead to the distant target. This approach will support the efforts of the student by guaranteeing that rewards will be available frequently and also to allow the student to see that he is progressing. When one knows that one's efforts are not in vain, but that one can see the progress and the results of the hard work, that in itself is a great motivator and a sense of satisfaction. There is a saying:

I'm not who I could be,
I'm not who I should be,
But I'm better than I was,
And I like the direction I'm going.

This speaks to students working at a level of *accomplishment* rather than at an *achievement* level of performance. This is also the kind of sentiment that students have when a well designed goal setting program is working for them.

It is often important, especially in pursuit of long term goals, to take some breaks along the way. This in itself could be a reward at a certain stage. The opportunity to engage in some other type of activity is necessary to prevent boredom and fatigue from entering and thus deterring the student.

And finally, celebrate! Your student is working hard and is accomplishing. When a certain criteria has been met, celebrate! Let the student know that you think he is doing great. Have some meaningful perk for the student. This is something else that the teacher and student can jointly discuss.

With Children

Two considerations need to be remembered when planning the goal setting trip with children:

1. Help them to plan the trip in a series of short stages so that there are a number of occasions when success and progress will be evident. Write it down on a plan or make a map of the journey to success.

2. Help them to sequence the steps so that each step is slightly more demanding than the previous. Each stage should be designed so that it is gradually directing the student closer to the long term goal.

For Success

The involvement of the teacher is critical for the success of a goal setting program. Teachers can be involved in a number of ways throughout the program. The following are some that will help to ensure success for the students:

1. Teachers must inform students that goals can be changed and revised. Often students will set goals that are beyond their capabilities. It is necessary however to let them try their wings, to make a mistake and learn from it. The next goal that they set will be much more realistic.

2. Teachers have the professional expertise to help students design a path toward a long term goal that is in a logical and sequential order. Sequencing tasks helps to avoid information and attention overload for the student. Throughout a term, students can be aided to focus on selected priority goals leading to the long term goal. This approach will help to ensure that each

step along the way is manageable for the student thereby making success more immediate and the development of a positive sense of self-esteem more likely.

3. Teachers can provide positive reinforcement for student's efforts and help the student to recognize the accomplishments that are being made. By keeping track of the gains that a student makes, this information is readily available to share with students and parents. Often students do not know what they have accomplished. It is difficult for students to be aware of changes they have made in areas such as reading or creative writing. The changes that do occur are often quite subtle. The teacher's role in this regard is vital. Inform the students as to what they have done. Feedback is the Breakfast of Champions (Blanchard and Johnson, 1985).

Step Four: Identify the Problems

Plan for the Road Blocks

One of the reasons so many people don't set goals for themselves is that they are afraid that others will make fun of their goals. We naturally avoid rejection and criticism. Students will feel the same way. To avoid this difficulty, the goals that are set should be confidential and only known by the teacher and the student involved.

Another problem with setting goals is that once set, a student is committed to a course of action. What if he fails? The fear of failure is so pronounced in some people that it actually paralyses them from any action in the direction of a desired goal. But often when this is the case, the only goal that is focused on is the one that is lofty, the one that is more

long term and difficult to achieve. Those people who become
overwhelmed by the fear of failure usually do not know the
principles behind a successful goal setting program. Making
students aware of small steps and showing them through
concrete examples that they can be successful, helps students
deal with obstacles to their goals in a realistic and manageable fashion.

Other road blocks that students may identify are in the
areas of their own behavior, their skill level, their attitude, the
time they have available to meet the goal and the resources
available to them. Teachers can discuss each concern with a
student so that difficulties can be addressed. It is important
that students begin the pursuit of their goals in a positive
frame of mind, a frame of mind that says "I can do it!"

Step Five: Plan the Detours

Deal with the Road Blocks

Once the difficulties of working toward a goal have been
identified, teacher and student together need to come up with
a strategy that addresses each problem. Giving students many
examples of how they can deal with an obstacle will help to
give students confidence in working in a new area.

Knowing the strengths of each student and planning the
strategy for obtaining the goal with this in mind will build
confidence and improve communication between the student
and teacher. When goals and behavioral expectations are
clear, students are more likely to be open and responsive
when communicating with one another and with their
teachers regarding progress and road blocks.

The process of careful and meaningful planning for goal
setting should not be thought of as something limited to those
with exceptional abilities. Students with low and intermediate

ability often have even greater payoffs in terms of accomplishment and enhancement of self-esteem. Goal setting is a means to ensure positive and satisfying personal development and increased participation in a learning environment.

Step Six: Set Time Lines

For best results, there are some considerations involving time lines that need to be addressed. It is important to set short range goals. These can be for one class period or less, for a day, week or month, depending upon the nature of the activity, the student and the level of development at the time the goal is set. There is an old saying: By the yard it's hard; by the inch it's a cinch. This means that taking things a little at a time can make it manageable. So it is with goal setting.

Setting goals that can be achieved in a relatively short period of time is important to morale and to give students a sense that they are capable of doing what they set out to do.

Time lines may vary for different goals. It is important to stress that establishing time lines like setting up goals is very individual. Each student needs goals that meet personal needs and abilities. Therefore it is impossible to prescribe a formula that applies in most cases. However, careful adherence to the principles outlined here make individualizing the program possible.

Setting lower level goals, that is goals that are relatively easy to accomplish or that are in a students area of strength is also a great morale booster.

Step Seven: Review

Plan to Review

Planning to set aside regular time when the teacher and student can review the progress that is being made is essential and an integral part of a goal setting plan. The opportunity for the student to see the progress that he is making is important for the development of positive self feelings. Imagine if you were in a situation where you worked many long and hard hours without knowing the progress you had made. It would be discouraging indeed. Yet for many students this is exactly the picture they face daily.

It is easy for someone who has no skill to see a change when some skill is acquired. For instance, a beginning reader who comes into a classroom situation not knowing any words can, after three or four months, read some basic sight words and have a real sense of accomplishment because he can recognize the change that he has made because of his own good efforts and persistence. However, a student who is reading at the grade four level, for instance, has a much more difficult time distinguishing the progress made. One difference is that at this level of reading, the changes that occur are far more subtle. Subtle to the point that it is difficult for a teacher to know exactly what kinds of specific progress have been made without careful and continual monitoring.

Most students really do not know and cannot state in concrete terms what their accomplishments are from one term to another. This can only harm the development of a positive self-image where school is concerned. So it follows then that frequent review of a student's progress toward a goal is critical.

The review can take many forms. Feedback may be verbal, written, a series of checklists, demonstration of a skill, anecdotal comments or charts. Teachers should try to combine a number of ways of providing this information to students so that they can relate to the message more successfully.

During the review time, students and teachers can introduce new ideas to be implemented, allow for some steps or goals to be revised, and provide feedback that primarily encourages students on to the next step in the program.

SUMMARY CHAPTER FIVE

1. Goals are dreams on a timeline.

2. When initially setting goals with children:
   a) goals should be short term
   b) goals should be easily attainable

3. Other factors to be considered when setting goals with children are:
   a) knowledge of the student's past performance must be considered when planning future performance strategies
   b) varying timelines should be considered in setting goals
   c) direction and specificity in the terminology used to write the goal is important for the success of the program
   d) goals must be measurable
   e) goals need to be appropriately challenging to provide the student with a sense of accomplishment when the goal is reached
   f) goals and the progress that is being made toward them must be under constant supervision. Modification of goals may be necessary to ensure success.

4. Seven steps when writing goals are:
   a) commit the goal to writing
   b) understand the goal
   c) develop a plan to attain the goals
   d) identify problems in attaining the goals
   e) strategies for dealing with the problems
   f) set a time line for implementation
   g) review/reassess the goals

6   Relaxation

Relaxation may well be the most important skill to master on the way to developing a new self-concept. Many people are so caught up with everyday tasks and all the associated life stresses that they have a hard time learning to slow these side effects down. Most are being pulled by several forces at a time. We must be aware of these stresses before we can begin to cope with them. Life's demands sap our energy and occupy parts of our consciousness so that we are largely unable to devote undivided attention to those things that are really important to us. Because we are caught up in the whirlwind of demands even when we are supposed to be resting, attention interfering experiences central to our consciousness effect our sleep patterns. A cycle of restless sleep and more stress causes even more restless sleep and more stress. Life becomes burdensome and difficult to handle.

At such times, it is easy to focus and dwell on negative thoughts and personal weaknesses. This process sets up a negative feedback loop inside our minds. The result is that we feel badly about ourselves or our performance which sets up a state of depression and increased anxiety. Such mood states may cause us to perform even more poorly and the cycle has begun again.

Learning to relax is a very effective method of handling this type of problem. Learning to relax also helps us learn to control our emotional environment that may otherwise control us. Patrick Fanning suggests that relaxation contributes significantly toward the reduction of anxiety, depression, anger, fear and obsessive thinking. When a person relaxes they produce Alpha waves. These waves are related to feelings of well-being, heightened awareness and an openness to positive suggestions. Ostrander and Schroeder in their book *Super-Learning* suggest that learning to relax not only helps individuals to control their emotional states but allows them to set up the first communication steps with the subconscious mind. From the perspective of making changes in the way we think and perceive ourselves, this link is critical. Relaxation is the first step to reaching those areas of our minds that contain our belief systems and our self-concepts. For those who would want to change the way they perceive themselves and modify their limiting beliefs about themselves, this skill is invaluable. Using relaxation techniques along with visualization (See Chapter 7) can make major differences in one's self perceptions.

There are a number of relaxation techniques that are very effective. Some common approaches and examples of effective methods will be presented so that a variety of techniques will be available for use. There is no need to use all of them. It may be found that one technique is more suitable than another for a given individual. Whatever proves to be most effective for an individual to get into the relaxed state is most appropriate. This implies that a number of trials with a number of different methods are attempted to determine a personal preference. Once a choice has been made, practicing this technique will bring about the relaxed state very quickly. With repeated practice over a number of days, entry into a relaxed state can occur in a matter of seconds.

Tension Awareness and Reduction

The first technique is a tension awareness and reduction exercise. This technique will aid in the reduction of body tension. As you do the exercise, become aware of the tension in your muscles and the relaxed state of your muscles. You will eventually be able to relax very tense muscles at will. Don't do these exercises so hard that you hurt yourself. To tense your muscles, do it firmly and gently avoiding abrupt flexions. Start by doing a little stretching and slowly rolling your head from side to side to prepare your muscles for exertion.

To begin, get into a comfortable position, either in a comfortable chair or laying on the floor. Adjust yourself so that you feel comfortable. Avoid crossing your legs on top of one another. As you relax, you may find the weight uncomfortable. Begin to become aware of your muscles and bones. Feel their weight. As you close your eyes take a slow, deep breath. Hold it for a moment and slowly exhale. As you exhale tell yourself to relax and feel the tension move out of your body. Take a second deep breath. Hold it. Now exhale and feel more tension leave your body. Replace the tense feeling with a warm relaxed feeling in your muscles. Feel your body becoming heavy as it relaxes. Take a third deep breath. Hold it. Exhale. Feel the beautiful feeling of relaxation starting to flow through your body. Enjoy this feeling.

Slowly tense the muscles of your legs. Tense the top of your legs, the calves and your toes. Hold it. Flex harder. Feel the tension in your muscles as you count slowly from one to five. Now relax. Feel the tension leaving and the relaxation taking over. Your legs feel heavy, warm and relaxed.

Focus on your lower leg and feet. Tense you lower leg and foot muscles. Count to five and slowly relax, feeling even more tension leave and more warmth and heaviness entering your muscles. Lay for a few seconds and enjoy the sensation of being relaxed.

Tense the upper part of your leg and lower leg and feet. Hold it. Tense a little more. Count from one to five. Now let go and relax. Feel your muscles relaxing. Pay attention to the sensation of tension and relaxation in your muscles. With every breath have tension flow out of your muscles as you exhale and feel a sense of relaxation flow in as you inhale.

Tense the muscles of your seat and hold it while you count to five. Let go and relax. Feel the tension leave your body. Feel the warmth, heaviness and relaxation. Warm, heavy and relaxed.

Move up to your lower back and abdomen. Tighten these muscles and hold the contraction. Pay attention to what the tension feels like. Flex harder as you count from one to five. Relax and let go. Feel the tension move out of your muscles. Become aware of the differences between a tensed muscle and a relaxed muscle. Move up to the upper part of your body. Tense you chest muscles, raise your shoulders back and toward your ears and tense your upper back. Take a deep breath and push out. Hold the tension hard while you slowly count to five. Become aware of the tension in your muscles. Now let go and relax. Feel your muscles become warm, heavy and relaxed.

Tense your arms and hands. Flex your muscles harder and harder. Hold and feel the tension as you count to five. Let go and relax. Feel the warmth, heaviness and relaxation enter your body as you breathe deeply. Focus on your upper arms, move to your forearms and then shift to your hands and feel the relaxation enter this part of your body. Let those muscles relax even more.

Tighten the muscles of your face. Squint your eyes. Tighten your lips, scalp, the muscles of your neck. Hold these as you count to five. Now let go and feel the warmth, heaviness and relaxation penetrate these muscles. Most people keep their tension in their face, scalp or neck. Tighten these muscles one more time. Make sure your throat, mouth and tongue are tensed. Hold for a slow count of five. Let all of those muscles get heavy, warm and relaxed.

Tense all of the muscles of your body, from your toes to the top of your scalp. Hold it for a count of five. Now let go and feel the wave of relaxation flow through you body. Feel your face, neck, chest, arms, stomach, seat, legs and arms relax.

Become aware of your state of relaxation. Let your mind go over your body to see it there are any tense areas. If you sense areas of tension flex those muscles. Hold them for a count of five and relax. Once done, enjoy the sensation and let it flow through your body. Waves of relaxation will flow through you. Relax and enjoy it. You deserve to feel as good as you do.

You are able to become what you would like to be. Repeat this to yourself, "I can be what I want to be." As you count backward from five to one you will open your eyes. You will feel refreshed and relaxed, tension free and full of energy, ready to tackle anything you are faced with.

The more you practice relaxation exercises the easier it will be for you to get into a relaxed state. Practice this several times so that you can move into a relaxed state easily. Once you know the system, practice it in several different areas. With more practice you'll be able to get into the relaxed state in a matter of seconds. Use it in your everyday life to help you concentrate and focus on your task.

Some authors (Fanning, 1988) have suggested that a condensed version of the above exercise can be practiced. Start by flexing each of the muscle groups mentioned earlier. Hold each of these for a couple of seconds and let go to let each of the groups relax. Once done let a wave of relaxation run down your entire body from head to toe. You should do two or three cycles of this tension relaxation series. Each relaxation cycle should take the time necessary to count to fifteen. Do these two or three times to get rid of the tension in your muscles from head to toe.

Visualization Relaxation Exercise

There are a number of other techniques that can be used to get people into states of relaxation. Albinson and Bull (1988) in their book *A Mental Game Plan* describes a visualization relaxation exercise. This is a different approach which may be more appropriate for your personality.

To begin, take a deep breath in through your mouth and nose. Hold it. Exhale passively. Begin to breathe slowly and deeply. Focus on your slow, deep abdominal breathing. Notice how each time you exhale you feel more relaxed. Close your eyes and continue to focus on your breathing. Picture yourself at the top of a long descending staircase. It seems to go down forever. See yourself beginning to move down the stairs. With each breath you descend down, down, down. With each step down you feel yourself become more and more relaxed. Down, relaxed. Relaxed, down. Continue down the staircase. When you feel you are totally relaxed and calm, you will find a landing. You can go there and enjoy the relaxed feeling until you hear the next instructions. At that time you will pay attention. Continue down, relaxing, down, relax. Pay attention to the following instructions.

You are relaxed, calm, and feeling good about yourself. On this landing, you will see a door. Open it. You will find behind it a place, a room, a situation which you find very relaxed and comfortable. It may be a warm bath, a room furnished as you would like it, a place in the country, or on a lake. Some place that will be your private place. It will be a place to enjoy. A place in which to feel totally relaxed, calm, comfortable and good about yourself. When you move through the door put yourself in a very comfortable position in your private place. Feel a wave of relaxation go through your body as you move into your place. Enjoy this place for a while and become very familiar with it. You will maintain a feeling of total relaxation while you are there. Enjoy this feeling for a while.

You may pay attention to the following instructions. Each time you do this exercise you will find that you can reach this place more quickly and feel more relaxed in it. When you are ready, bring yourself back to a state of full alertness. Counting back from ten to one, bending and stretching your arms a couple of times, moving your head from side to side, opening your eyes and then you will feel awake, alert, relaxed and calm and feeling good about yourself.

When you are reading the above exercise you will have to pause where it is appropriate. A pause of at least ten seconds between each sentence is expected. Some areas require a pause of up to 30 seconds. Another good source of relaxation exercises is a book called, *Superlearning* by Ostrander and Schroeder (1979). Other valuable sources will be books on Sports Psychology.

Learning to Relax

1. You should practice every day using any technique that is effective for you.

2. In the beginning it may help if you use some of the exercises that have been described. Eventually you will have to learn how to get the relaxation response by yourself. You may start with tape recordings you buy (e.g., Bach's Brandenberg Concerto No. 4, 2nd movement; Bach's Orchestral Suite no.2; or Holst's The Planets Venus; Ravel's Mother Goose Suite, 1st movement) or you may take the above exercises you have read or found somewhere else you like and make a recording with your own voice.

3. A good way to make these exercises even more relaxing is to add music to the program. There are a number of tapes available that have specially selected musical arrangements that are known to be relaxing. If you are going to use music of your own, make sure you select pieces that have no emotions attached to them. If there is an emotional attachment, every time you hear the music, those emotions will come up so strongly, that you will dwell upon them, not on relaxation.

4. Some people fall asleep when they relax. This could be a problem. The point of doing the exercises is to bring about a state of calm but yet alertness so one can perform at their best. You should say to yourself, "even though I am very relaxed I will stay awake and alert." Some authors suggest that you hold your lower arm up so if you fall asleep you will be awakened when it falls. Any signal that keeps you awake will be helpful if you have this problem.

5. You should be checking yourself out to make sure you are going into a relaxed state. You could have

someone else check you out by lifting an arm to see if it is relaxed. A good check is to develop an awareness inside yourself to sense any tension or tightness. Once you know the sensation of relaxation you can be aware when you are in it.

6. When you are practicing your relaxation techniques, try to get into the state as quickly as possible and as deeply as possible. A suitable statement you repeat several times may be all that is required. For example, you may simply need only say, "I am calm, relaxed and in control."

7. Learn a backup method if for some reason one technique does not work as anticipated on a given day. You will find that as you learn to get your relaxation response quickly it will be easier and easier to move into it. The key is to learn to sense how you feel and to become aware how you respond when you are under stress and how you feel when you are relaxed. Everyone's response will be different. Learn what works for you.

SUMMARY CHAPTER SIX

1. The ability to relax at will is a necessary skill to preparing the brain to accept new perceptions required to develop a modified self-concept.

2. There are a number of effective strategies that can be used to relax. One may work better for a given individual than another. What is most important is that one approach is mastered and that the student has the faith to rely on this approach when relaxation is needed.

7 Visual and Mental Rehearsal

What the mind can conceive and the heart believe, can be achieved.   -- *Napoleon Hill*

"What you see is what you get!"   -- *Flip Wilson*

Introduction

Slogans!? Maybe. But in the field of business and industry, and in the athletic arenas around the world, peak performers share one common quality. They can visualize themselves doing things that have never been done before.

On another level, they are accomplishing personal firsts. When we set out to better ourselves, or improve our situation in life, we must go beyond the familiar, that which we are currently doing. This involves risk and setting out into the *personal unknown*. But risk we must. Second base cannot be stolen if we are insistent on keeping our foot planted on first. To advance, we must risk. But more important, to advance, we must believe that we can be successful. We must be able to see ourselves doing that which we desire. This is visualization.

While the terminology and the conscious control of thoughts for personal betterment may seem foreign to many, visualization is quite natural and something in which we all engage daily.

In the 1990's, mental imagery and visualization is employed in a wide variety of areas ranging from physical healing and health, and problem solving to strategic planning, performance enhancement, learning and retention. The knowledge that has led to the widespread use of visualization has been available for many years. In 1960, Maxwell Maltz wrote in *Psycho-cybernetics* that imagination is not something reserved for poets, philosophers and inventors. It enters into our every act. Imagination sets the visual picture of our goal which directs the automatic mechanism toward that end. We act, or fail to act, not because of *will*, as is so commonly believed, but because of vivid imagination, the catalyst of positive action.

In fact, a more challenging question might be to ask "How does one not visualize?"

In January when the winter winds are blowing at our windows, we can successfully imagine ourselves laying on a beach in some tropical paradise basking in the sun. We can visualize how a room will look before we rearrange the furniture. We can see a friend's face in our mind or imagine a rose resting in a vase on a table. For those of us who have experienced winter driving, the vivid image of attempting to stop our car on an icy road only to realize that we are too close to the car in front of us is a chilling thought indeed. This image can cause us to break out in a cold sweat when we vividly imagine.

In our everyday conversations with friends, we use mental images to assist us in communicating. Such phrases as.. *imagine that...*, *picture this...*, and *I see...* are commonly used by us all. The entertainment value that one derives from buying a lottery ticket is found almost exclusively in the visualizations that one has because of the possibilities of *winning the big one!*

Clearly, visualization is something that we do frequently. The application of this mental skill can work to our advantage or to our disadvantage. What is necessary, is for us to learn how to derive positive benefits from this process and consistently apply this skill to help us reach personal goals.

Brief Findings from the Research

It should be noted that mental rehearsal and visualizations are not a substitute for active practice and directed action. Mental training can be used successfully to augment active skill development that has preceded it.

Mental rehearsal is beneficial because physiologically, it allows a firing of the neural pathways that are actually involved in the physical performance of the practiced skills.

When a person practices any new skill, be it swimming, public speaking or reading, neural pathways are gradually opened which with repeated practice become entrenched as the way in which one performs a given skill. Over time, as the skill improves, one develops a memory of how the skill *feels* when it is performed in a given way. Ideally, when one gets to the point of performing the skill well, the feeling of a good performance is the one that is retained. Recent research however has indicated that our nervous system cannot tell the difference between a vividly imagined experience and a *real* experience. The key is in the vividness of the images created. This will be discussed in more detail later in this chapter. However, in both cases, the nervous system responds as if what you think or imagine is true. You act, and feel, not according to what things are really like, but in accordance to the image your mind holds of what things are like.

Research Quarterly reported an experiment conducted with basketball players and the use of mental rehearsal. In the study, college level basketball players were divided into three groups and pretested shooting foul shots. Following this,

Group One was asked not to engage in any form of basketball activity for one month. Group Two was asked to come into the gym every day for a month and practice throwing foul shots. Group Three was directed to come to the gym each day and stand at the foul line and vividly imagine themselves successfully sinking foul shots.

At the conclusion of the experiment, all three groups were tested again. As one might expect, the group that had not practiced had scores that actually declined in accuracy. Group Two, who had physically practiced shooting each day had scores that improved by 24 percent. The players in Group Three, who had only practiced in their imagination had an improved score of 23 percent. Almost identical to the group who had physically prepared!

What was occurring in the two successful groups was that through practice, neural pathways were opening to ensure a consistent standard of performance in the future. The difference was in the manner by which the neural pathways were opened, not so much in the results. In the absence of actual practice or action, mental rehearsal is a way of literally programming mental circuits. What has been demonstrated so clearly for years in the world of sport, has also been documented in academics and business.

This effect has been called the *Carpenter effect*. Through mental stimulation, neurological patterns are facilitated which produce an improved efficiency of both future images and performed actions.

The major types of mental imagery and the various applications of these major types will now be examined. Guidelines on how to successfully use mental imagery will also be discussed.

MAJOR CATEGORIES OF MENTAL IMAGERY

Mental imagery is typically divided into two main categories in the literature, namely, *dissociative* and *associative* imagery.

In general, dissociative means that we dis-associate our thoughts from what is actually occurring at a given time. We try to distance ourselves from a given place or time by imagining a substitute experience. We literally attempt to *space out* or get away from reality. Associative imagery on the other hand allows us to focus more intently on what is presently occurring to us and to better control our reactions to expected conditions. Kubistant (1986) prefers to use the term disassociative rather than dissociative for purposes of its descriptive ability. This author will follow that pattern as well, hopefully to assist the reader.

Disassociative Imagery

Daydreaming, singing a song in your mind, and creating or recreating a pleasant event in one's mind are common forms of disassociative imagery. It is a form of concentration distraction from reality. In this form, the concentration that a person is having is not related to the performance at hand, but it is a means of intentionally *closing the door* on an experience or event. For example, a swimmer engaged in a distant swim may let her mind wander to a variety of images to avoid the boredom that can set in over time in this form of exercise. Students too, engage in disassociative imagery when they daydream as a means of escaping from the reality of working on homework. This form of imagery can be used to temporarily avoid reality or to relive a pleasant memory.

To believe that disassociative imagery is used only as a means of escape would be to sell it short. More constructively, this form of disassociating allows the mind to become clear of images that hamper creativity. Visualizing calm and peaceful scenes from nature have been found beneficial to assist students to deal with worries and distractions that can otherwise create blocks to learning. Disassociative imagery as Ostrander and Schroeder (1979) have pointed out helps to establish a link between the conscious and unconscious parts of the brain. By calming the mind, constructive images can more effectively be delivered.

Just telling yourself statements such as *I learn easily* or *I remember perfectly* is not enough. Calming both your body and your mind help to establish a more conducive atmosphere for effectively using mental imagery. This was discussed in greater detail in Chapter 6, (Relaxation Techniques).

The courier that is most effective in delivering the message to the unconscious mind is emotion. Recapturing the feeling of a successful experience and substituting this feeling and applying it to the current challenge is the key to effective visualization. Disassociative imagery coupled with relaxation helps to lay the ground work.

Disassociative imagery, while often a pleasant experience in itself, often sets the stage for associative imagery. To be able to associate directly and with the greatest effect, it is necessary to clear the mind of distractions that may interfere with constructive images attaining their desired impact. Disassociative imagery serves this purpose.

Associative Imagery

Associative imagery is a form of concentration that focuses on task relevant cues which are directly related to performance. To use the analogy of tuning in a radio to receive a clearer signal from a distant station may help to understand the function of this form of mental rehearsal. Associative imagery allows us to *tune in* to our mind and body. It is associative imagery that is often referred to as *visualization.*

Visualization is a controlled and directed form of imagery. It implies controlling the image and directing it to the desired positive results. Whether the application is to increase the rate of healing in a pulled muscle, seeing a crowd respond positively to you when you present an oral presentation, or accurately recalling information, associative imagery acts as a catalyst to facilitate and build confidence in one's physical and mental abilities.

When people exercise recreationally, it is not uncommon to see them with a cassette player or pocket radio plugged into their ears. This is a form of disassociative behavior because it helps to relieve the athlete from the monotony that sometimes accompanies activities such as cycling or jogging. This is quite different from the practices that elite performers engage in.

The elite in any activity *tune in*...associate...with their bodies and their minds. They become acutely aware of how their bodies are feeling at different stages of an activity and they learn to interpret these signs, forms of biofeedback, as one would a map. Their bodies are speaking to them about fatigue and strain. Their minds are speaking to them about anxiety or boredom. The elite performers in all fields will notice these signs and be able to respond to them with appropriate associative imagery so that the performance is not adversely effected.

For instance, a public speaker, prior to giving an address may experience *butterflies* before being introduced to the audience. This can be devastating! One could react by noticing the anxiety level continue to skyrocket. Or one could say, "Good! Those butterflies are a sign that I'm ready...I'm up for this one!" How one has prepared to deal with this inevitable feeling dictates the nature of the response when the butterflies are first noticed. However, the visualizations that the speaker has while preparing for the presentation is key to determining the nature of the response in practice.

In another example, a graduate student preparing to defend a thesis may be overwhelmed by the prospect. This is not a unique experience by any means. Imagine this scenario. You are a student who has just worked for three years taking courses, doing research and preparing for this one final exam. All of the past effort hinges on how well you have prepared and on how well you present yourself and your work to your academic superiors. How will you do? Will you become nervous and forget key points? Will you become confused explaining a difficult concept? Ultimately will you be successful, or will it all be for not?

These are questions that most graduate students grapple with at some time. Some resolve them. Others don't and go into a thesis defense in as nervous a state as possible. However, this need not be the case! If one were to prepare for the oral examination by visualizing positive scenes where the defendant is in control of the situation, the anxiety levels will dramatically decrease. Unrealistic you say! Not at all!

Probably no one else in the room at the time of the defense is as well versed on the research as the defending student. No one else has worked so closely with the project as the student. And no one else has been privy to the background for why certain decisions were made that led to the final product as the student. A student should feel at ease also because going into the examination, the student's advisors have already indicated that the student and the work are ready for the final defense stage. This should indicate to the student that even before the exam begins, there is a substantial body of support for the student in existence already.

This sort of background information when realized can greatly assist a student to create positive mental images, supportive visualizations about one's performance during the time of the examination itself.

Visualizing can also be beneficial during a performance. Being aware of subtle changes in perspiration, rate of breathing, etc., can be the cues that a person responds to when reconstructing a positive image. This awareness greatly supports the person who is attempting to successfully complete the task at hand. Visualization can have three functions. It can assist a person:

a) in being more aware of ourself at various times during a performance

b) in controlling the adjustments that may need to be made during a performance

c) in preparing for a performance by helping to preset certain mental images in support of actual performance skills

It should be noted that both disassociative and associative imagery are important and can be successfully used to improve performance in any area. It should also be noted that visualization is a supplement to other forms of performance improvement and is not a substitute for them.

FACTORS AFFECTING THE EFFECTIVENESS
OF MENTAL REHEARSAL

Mental rehearsal can be an effective tool for a student if its practice follows certain guidelines:

1. *The vividness of the images*

The imagery should be as clear and as vivid as possible. Sufficient physical practice in an event or performance area is a pre-requisite to effective mental rehearsal. The images should compliment what has been physically practiced. Vivid *key words* or phrases will greatly assist in constructing a clear image that will be easily retained and recalled by the student. Asking a student to remember sounds, colors and textures that may add to the vividness of the image may be helpful.

It is also important to recall clearly the objectives of the performance. These two elements (clear objectives or goals and sufficient time actually practising) have been shown to greatly assist students in creating vivid images in their mind.

2. *Control of the imagery*

The imagery must also be controlled according to the individual's needs and according to the requirements of the task. The image should not only be vivid and persistent, but the student should also be able to halt the image at any time during the mental training. Occasionally a person sees himself performing a skill incorrectly. This image needs to be halted. As an alternate, the student needs to see himself being able to handle the faulty performance and then see himself correcting the action.

3. *Clear directives*

Objectives for specific situations must be clearly defined in order for mental rehearsal to be effective. This relates directly to what the student goals are for a given training session. Success in the mental training depends on having clearly defined, attainable and realistic goals...a reason for the training!

4. *Proper focus of attention*

The focus on the relevant components of a task constitutes an essential element for effective mental rehearsal. Associative imagery can be used to anticipate events before, during and after a performance. When used to anticipate an activity, mental rehearsal can be used as a preliminary strategy helping a student to focus on the task and control pre-performance anxiety. It can also be used to achieve an optimal level of appropriate attention for the task at hand. In being able to see oneself in control of a situation, positive expectations are developed which can have a motivational effect by developing a desire to do well. Visualizing personal strategies for dealing with a situations also aids in this regard.

5. *The perspective of imagery*

The research reports two perspectives of imagery within which one can mentally evoke the sensory aspects of a performance. The two are external and internal imagery.

External

The analogy of watching yourself on television would most closely describe the phenomena of external imagery. One imagines that one is watching a performance from the view point of a spectator. We literally see ourselves from the outside.

It is a common practice to use video equipment to provide feedback to performers. This assists in the development of external imagery, imagery from the spectator point of view.

Internal

With internal imagery, the performer actually does the activity. There is a kinesthetic quality about the image in that the person can feel the way the performance would feel if it were being performed. Everything happens in the mind as the performer sees himself performing as if he was in a live performance.

While external imagery is valuable for skill enhancement and sequencing actions, the internal perspective is applied for more precision and refined actions involving both gross and fine motor control. It needs to be noted however that both are useful. One needs to be able to visualize an activity to be performed externally and then fuse the internal visualization with the former. Having both types of visualizations enhances the total performance. Key sensations and it *feels like* internalizations help the individual perform by giving identifiable reactions that enables enhanced performance to occur.

Athletically it is quite easy to feel reactions within your body. For example, high jumpers speak of having their chests lift high over the bar to get enough elevation. The athlete has an outward visualization of what the skill looks like which is used to develop the overall skill synaptically. Now what is needed are internal check points that allow the person to feel whether the performance is good. This involves becoming aware of key moves in the whole performance. With many successful performances, these internal check points become the focus points to help the individual get into *the grove*. The same phenomenon operates in any type of activity.

People who are public speakers use these same techniques to get themselves ready to perform well. There are internal check points we all use to determine if we are close to the level we would like to perform at.

These techniques have been used in schools to develop research skills and write good papers. The students are taught the techniques they need and are coached along the way to feel key check points that gets the student to perform well.

Musicians are using this technique to improve performance. They are asked to visualize themselves performing both externally and internally. Eventually using the previously mentioned techniques, performance does improve.

It is interesting to note that while peak performers indicate that internal imagery is the most effective in enhancing personal performance, the pedagogical tool that is most frequently used to help create images is the video camera, a tool that favors the development of external imagery. Teachers and coaches need to be aware of this contradiction when they prepare to work to enhance performance in any field. New strategies employed by teachers need to focus on enabling participants to improve their mental abilities to use internal visualization.

In teaching reading for example, it is often effective to encourage students to mentally enter the scene described in the book. This activity can help students to comprehend the reading selection. In teaching creative writing for instance, if the topic to be considered was *Knights*, a pre-writing activity to visualize the environment might be suggested. If students could imagine themselves entering the castle in medieval times, visualizing the room, the feeling associated with that place and then see a sequence of events unfold, a large creative portion of the writing process would have been completed. Then, encourage the students to record these images on paper. This is a very effective strategy indeed!

WHEN TO MENTALLY REHEARSE

The two main benefits of mental rehearsal are 1) that it prepares the mind and body for an upcoming activity, and 2) it can be used as the main tool for maintaining performer attention to factors that are relevant to an approaching task. There are several occasions when mental rehearsal can be most beneficial:

1. Mental rehearsal can be used when a skill or series of skills are already being performed well and consistently. Encouraging students to actively imagine those skills being performed successfully can be used as a valuable support technique to actual training or practice.

For example, a student preparing to have a role in a stage production might externally visualize where she would stand on the stage and where and when she would move during a performance. Internally, the same actress might experience the buildup of an emotion required to convincingly role play a certain scene. Being able to summon an emotional response at will is a good example of a practical use of this form of mental rehearsal.

2. Mental rehearsal can be successfully used as the last performer-controlled activity prior to actually performing. Again, calling upon emotional feeling or arousal helps the performer to narrow the focus of attention so that a state of attention closely matching the performance state can be achieved.

3. When skills are being performed that extend over long periods of time, it is often impractical to visualize the entire performance. However, key points need to be reinforced. Examples of key points might be:

a) a counter argument to a likely point made by one's opponent during a debate

b) dealing with the onset of intense contractions and pain during the delivery of a newborn (This is a male point of view...please screen if necessary)

c) a football quarterback might visualize how a second strategy might be implemented when the set play is fouled up by the opposing defense

4. Mental rehearsal is part of thorough preparation for an upcoming event, be it in the arts, athletics or academics. Planning one's strategy for a forthcoming event should be part of wise preparatory procedures. Visualizing movement patterns or suspected obstacles that might interfere with one's performance is required for adequate preparation to control pre-event anxiety. Imagining how one will respond to those obstacles is also necessary to reduce a performers anxiety and is an important use of mental imagery.

5. For many activities which require repetition and/or are predictable, for instance, giving an oral presentation, recalling the procedures to solve problems, or understanding relationships between phenomena, mental rehearsal makes it possible to concentrate on perfecting the performance that is anticipated. Prior to a performance, it has been found that mental rehearsal that focuses on recall and the actual performance should receive most of the preparatory time, with less time, approximately 20 percent, being devoted to coping strategy. That is, how will the performer cope when difficulties begin to occur during the performance.

For instance, if a student is doing an oral book report in front of her classmates, prior to making the presentation, the student should spend most of her time visualizing what she will say and how she will say it, and less time on how she will react if the class looks bored. This is not to suggest that class reaction is a trivial concern. Far from it! But attention to performing well will reduce class boredom, will be the primary factor for positive recognition from the teacher, and should be the main student focus in preparation. Having a strategy which deals with a disinterested audience is a proactive stance and should be confronted as part of sound preparation. However, the main focus on preparation must be the presentation itself!

HOW TO MENTALLY REHEARSE

Many situations exist where the exact response from the environment, be it natural or man made are unpredictable. Situational circumstances where varying numbers of alternatives exist confound the best of preparation attempts. However, mental preparation is still possible and advisable. The performer needs to direct attention toward cues which are relevant to the activity. Attention to irrelevant thoughts about one's self or the environment can be sources of distraction from the task and can be a cause of a lower quality of performance.

Like other skills, mental rehearsal is learned. Practice of this skill improves its effectiveness. What follows are key features to be addressed by people who want to fully utilize the power of mental rehearsal.

1. The main objective of skill imagery is to involve all the senses so that one can see and feel a flawless performance. This vivid form of imagery initiates a

slight firing of the neural pathways that will be used when an actual performance is done. Imagery helps to establish a positive performance pattern.

2. To begin, relax! Then visualize simple and familiar images, images of a performance that can already be done well. Have the student get the *feel* for that action. Set aside about five minutes a day to recapture the mental image at will.

3. With practice, the mental rehearsal will ideally begin to involve all the senses. Have the student imagine the place where the action will take place. See the lighting in the room, the arrangements of the desks, the location of other people within this setting. Imagine what the room looks like, how it smells, the temperature in the room, how the room *feels* when you walk into it, i.e., does anxiety build when one walks into the room or even imagines the facility. Try to have the student imagine successfully doing some activity within this environment.

4. Over time, gradually increase the complexity of the images and the amount of time devoted to visualizing. **Remember, mental rehearsal is not daydreaming!** Mental rehearsal is controlling one's thoughts and it employs vivid images that involve all the senses. It takes practice! The ultimate objective of visualization is to experience an act using the senses through internal stimulation.

5. Imagery is a polysensory process. The more senses that can be stimulated through imagery, the more vivid and intense the images will be. The more vivid the

images, the more benefit one can expect from this form of preparation.

Productive mental rehearsal allows the imager to manipulate the images so that increasingly they are approaching the desired goal. Images need to be controlled. For example, one student attempted to see herself as increasingly popular with her classmates. However, in her imagination she could not see herself approaching a group of children without beginning to feel anxious. In her imagination she could not get beyond this image. This was a very vivid image for her! Vividness was not enough to build the confidence required to reach her goal. Her inability to control the image and see herself successfully interacting with her peers disrupted her concentration and did not help her improve her interaction patterns.

SUMMARY CHAPTER SEVEN

1. Neural pathways are opened by both active practice and through mental rehearsal.

2. Both disassociative imagery and associative imagery or visualization can be used to enhance student performance.

3. Factors affecting the effectiveness of mental rehearsal are:

   a) the vividness of the images

   b) control of the imagery

   c) a clear purpose for engaging in the mental rehearsal

   d) the perspective of the imagery

8 The Winning Feeling

Our BELIEF SYSTEM, as explained in Chapter 4, is a psychological filter through which individuals view the world and their role in it. Our BELIEF SYSTEM is a learned phenomena, a subcomponent of the self-concept. As our self concept develops, we learn who we are and what we believe to be our level of competency, or our BELIEF SYSTEM. This system, a processing structure, has been established partly due to a synthesis of experiences, in combination with an accompanying emotional response that becomes connected or anchored to those experiences. Many human beliefs are held not because of a great deal of rational information but rather because of the emotions that are attached to the experiences. We all have beliefs that we feel are true, not because we can defend them with empirical data but because of the emotions attached to them. We feel comfortable or uncomfortable with a situation or person because of the emotions associated with an event or person. Because emotions are instrumental in anchoring what we believe to be true, we must pay particular attention to them. Beliefs are held more strongly if there are emotions attached to them. The stronger the emotions, the more intensely we hold on to our beliefs.

Dealing with one's self-esteem forces us to investigate the acquisition of beliefs. If we are to enhance a person's self-esteem, we need to know the process of change. There are two ways by which people can modify their Belief System: through Reframing and through Significant Emotional Events.

Reframing

The process of changing the way a person perceives his world is called *reframing*. Giving a new frame to the context of a situation or behavior does not change the behavior of anyone involved, it simply changes the frame in which the behavior occurred. The result of this is to change the perception of the behavior and therefore the significance of that behavior. For example, in a high school setting, a student was called into the office by the principal and suspended for behavior that was inconsistent with the expectations of the school. The principal also told the student that he had to complete all of the class assignments for the week and hand an essay in when he returned. The student left the office and immediately went to see the school counselor.

"If that so and so thinks that I'm going to do any work he's crazy, especially now that I'm suspended." After a few minutes of blowing off steam, the student finally settled down. The counselor asked him if he would really like to get back at the principal who so unjustly suspended him.

"You bet, I'm not going to do the work he expects. That'll show him. He can't push me around like that."

"What do you think the principal expects you to do?" asked the counselor. The student thought for a while and couldn't come up with an answer. "Do you think the principal expects the work to be done?"

"I'm not going to do any work for that SOB, and that's final. He can't push me around."

"I asked you earlier if you would like to get back at him? If you do, let me tell you how I see the principal reacting. He expects you not to do the work so that he can come into the staff room and show the staff that you reacted the way he expected. If you really want to nail the principal, let's make him look as bad as he expects you to look."

"What do you mean?" asked the student.

"What if you did the work better than the principal expected. What could he say about you later? He couldn't run you down or make fun of you. You would really be getting back at him. Let's nail him instead of him nailing you."

The student jumped up and said what a good idea it was. A week later when the student returned, his work was completed so well, everyone, including the principal commended him for work well done. The counselor reframed the situation so that both the student and principal were eventually satisfied with the student's behavior. Incidentally, the student was commended so much for his work he began to feel good about himself so that strong positive emotions became associated with school. He began to work hard and he ended up graduating from the high school with honors.

Significant Emotional Event

The second method of change is that of a *significant emotional event*. A significant emotional event is an event that affects a person so much that it changes the way the person perceives their world. In other words, the individual's Belief System is modified because of the intensity of the emotions attached to the situation or behavior. Some of these significant events are very dramatic in their effects on the person. Because of the strong emotions attached to the behavior, the emotions and the behavior become anchored to each other. This is a phenomena often discussed in Neuro-Linguistic literature. They are linked in such a way that every time a person thinks about or is in the same situation, the strong emotions are felt again. The significant emotional event can be as a result of an international situation viewed by many people at one time, or it can be the result of an event in a person's life that has a profound effect. There are many individuals who watched the visit of J.F. Kennedy in Dallas and sat in horror as they saw his body riddled by several bullets. Those who did see the event can remember in very specific detail where they were, what they were doing, what they were wearing and many other bits of information surrounding the event. That was a significant emotional event for all concerned. It was an event that will remain in the minds of those who saw it for most, if not all of their lives. We also experience significant emotional events that effect us as individuals and cause us to alter our Belief Systems. They do not have to be as dramatic as an assassination to be effective in causing an effect.

An individual may remember the reason why he feels the strong emotions he experiences, but it is more likely that he feels the emotions and is unable to understand why. Whether it is understood or not is not important. What is important is emotions are anchored to things, people, events or situations and cause us to react in reflexive ways that may or may not be desirable. If the significant emotional events are positive, the outcome or effect on our Belief System will be different than if they are negative. If the events are positive in a person's life, chances are that the individual has positive self-esteem. Our main concern is with individuals who are limited by poor self-esteem. One of the most frustrating experiences a parent or a teacher can have is to deal with someone who functions below his ability level. It seems as if these individuals sabotage their own progress and growth. If it were possible to control the occurrence of a significant emotional event in a positive way, an important first step would have been taken to changing a person's behavior and his feelings about himself. The exciting news is that it is possible!

The major criteria for successful programs for use in school or the home would be permanency of change and ease in learning the change techniques. Using strong psychological principles that have been successfully used in athletics and industrial settings, research has shown that a strong emotional component must be included when attempting to modify a person's Belief System. As mentioned earlier, strong emotions cause beliefs to be more firmly entrenched in our minds. Changes occur more readily if strong emotions are linked to the new behaviors. Sports psychologists have used the term *winning feeling* to describe what they believe is the necessary element athletes must associate with or bond to the new skill or performance level in order to be successful. Neuro-Linguists suggest that a strong anchoring of emotional states to new behavior is necessary to effect permanent change. The techniques that will be described have been proven effective with *at-risk* students in secondary schools over a three year period of controlled research. This is in addition to the numerous studies conducted in a wide variety of areas other than education.

Belief Systems develop over time as life experiences become internalized. People quickly learn what to expect from life and what is expected of them. In establishing a BELIEF SYSTEM, intense emotions have been attached to events, situations or to the individual in these roles. High levels of emotion are needed to effect change as well. This is especially true if the changes are to have any permanency.

Once learned, an individual will have the skills necessary to continue reinforcing changes that have already occurred.

The *Winning Feeling* is an intense emotional high that accompanies a sense of accomplishment, a sense of being someone special or a sense of being at ease with oneself. The experiences don't have to come from earth moving experiences or be so influential as to have made the national newspaper. Most *Winning Feelings* come from the day to day activities that are experienced. They are accomplishments and achievements that make us feel good about ourselves. Usually these feelings are personal and have significance only to the individual who perceives them to be important. That person remembers the event for a life time while it may have played such little significance to those around that person, that they didn't perceive the event as actually happening. It may have been a look, a word, a touch or the absence of all of the possible responses that cause an emotional response in the individual. If one reflects, that feeling can be brought back with a thought so that one can relive the experience and the emotion that went with it. The emotions may be linked to a time when one was the most creative, innovative, perceptive, loving, empathetic, etc. It was this event that caused the individual to feel powerful and in control of the situations he was in.

In order to make changes in a Belief System, one needs to bring back those *Winning Feelings* and bond them with a new behavior...the anchoring process. Anchoring involves an association between thoughts, ideas, feelings or states to a specific stimulus. The stimulus and the state become neurologically linked. For example, a teacher whose mother had passed away recently was given flowers from a student's home as a present. The teacher thanked her and put the flowers in a vase, placing them on her desk. The fragrance of the flowers began to permeate throughout the classroom. Suddenly the teacher became very upset emotionally and had to leave the classroom to compose herself. When she thought about it later, she realized that it was the fragrance of the flowers that had become associated or anchored to the strong emotions she experienced because of her mother's death. The fragrance of the flowers triggered the same emotional response that she had during her mother's funeral.

Similarly, many students *freeze up* during exams. In class, their performance would not indicate that they would have difficulty writing exams. However, most of these students would verbalize that they had always had trouble writing exams. Strong emotions of failure and lack of success had been anchored to writing exams. Students who have experienced past failure often project this feeling into future situations. Sitting down at a desk with examination paper and a pencil triggers the same emotions that have been associated in the past with a lack of success.

All teachers have known students who *knew* they wouldn't succeed. The typical teacher response is to give all kinds of evidence to show them that they can be successful. Students nod in agreement and teachers think they are convincing them to take a new stand and get down to work at a level of which they are capable. Sadly, however, nothing changes. More supportive evidence is given to convince the students that they are not perceiving the world the way they should. Frustrated teachers! Disbelieving students! Whose perception is correct? For performance to change, the student's perception is critical. Something more than evidence is needed to change a BELIEF SYSTEM.

Enter the Winning Feeling

Learning this skill of bringing about the *winning feeling* at will will begin to give the individual control over himself rather than letting his emotional states be governed by external influences. Emotions trigger whole patterns of thinking. Maxwell Maltz in his book *Psychocybernetics* says that our thinking develops in patterns called engrams These are whole series of neurons that are synaptically linked into patterns of thinking. Earlier it was stated that emotions drove these patterned thinking responses into stronger networks. If changes are to occur, learning to control emotions to relearn a new set of responses is necessary. Emotional control skills need to be taught so that optimal emotional responses can be present to facilitate synaptic linking. Some background may be necessary at this point.

Within our brain is a something called the Reticular Activating System. When we are experiencing an emotional high, the Reticular Activating System produces neuro-transmitters at a more abundant rate than in a non-emotional state. Physiologically, the brain does not function at its best without an abundance of neurotransmitters, and without an abundance of emotion. Literature on positive thinking says that thinking positively will produce good results. Neuro-psychologists suggest that one must feel good about oneself first because it is difficult to produce good results when you are not feeling your best. Positive thinking alone will not help to move an individual to a desired emotional state necessary to perform optimally.

Most people have been in a state where they felt terrific and did wonderful work. These times could be described as the most creative and productive. Answers came easily and ideas seemed to arrive effortlessly. In order to be in that state, one must feel good so that one can respond in a positive physiological manner. This state allows the body to produce neurotransmitters at optimal levels for peak performance. Assisting people to move into the Winning Feeling will establish the most productive mind-body (psychosomatic) connections. Not only will a productive state occur, but an association of behavior or situation with those good feelings will also occur. This sets up an opportunity for success to reoccur.

Links or associations do not always have to be attached to the most profound experiences. Ordinary life situations have been anchored to the need of action or the need to avoid a situation. For example, there are students who only do well when they are *under pressure.* They'll say, "I only do well on essays when they are due the next morning." Creativity has been linked with the pressure of deadlines. These people have a great deal of difficulty being creative and productive until deadlines loom. When pressure mounts, they kick into their productive mode. Productivity is clearly possible at other times as well. However, creativity and production have been anchored to the emotional anxiety of a deadline.

Similarly, some athletes are known as *clutch players.* They are players who repeatedly come off the bench to pull their teams from the brink of defeat, playing optimally when under pressure. They have anchored high quality play to the emotion of the threat of defeat.

Getting the Winning Feeling

Before a person can recall and then relive the winning feeling he may have to learn to relax (see ch. 6) enough to allow himself to remember the emotions of a high performance state. If individuals are having trouble getting into a relaxed state, they can be taught a progressive relaxation technique. This technique can be used to calm themselves down enough to let their experience of the winning feeling invade their being.

Step One

When working with students in the initial stages of calling up the winning feeling ask them to remember a time when they felt very good about themselves. It may have been a personal best in athletics, a time when they solved a problem in class that no one else could, or when they successfully completed a personal goal that made them stretch themselves to the limit. The particular event doesn't have to be outstanding in relationship to the accomplishments of others. So long as the event they are thinking about brings the memory of a winning feeling, this is the first step to learning this skill. Some students may have no experiences they can call upon to help them learn the skill. When this is the case, they should be asked to try to feel what it would be like if they did have a winning feeling. Encourage them to recall the winning feeling. Have them develop the most vivid picture of the event possible to enable them to feel how they felt when the event actually occurred. Students should be instructed to attempt to recall, in addition to the feeling, memories of that event using all of the senses.

It is beneficial to incorporate auditory, visual and kinesthetic processes when students practice the mental exercise of recalling their winning feeling. In order to return to the winning state, some of the following questions may be used to assist:

- What was the overall feeling like?
- Were you emotionally excited?

- Did you have goose bumps?
- Did you feel powerful or in control?
- As you begin to relive the winning feeling, take some time to let the experience flood your being.
- Were there any sounds that stand out?
- Were you saying any words or singing a song?
- Was there any music playing at the time?

If there were any of the above sounds, listen to them in your mind. Was there a particular sound associated with the winning feeling? The sound may have been a saying like *yes* or *yahoo*. The sound may also have been a deep guttural sound like a grunt that tennis players make when they hit a ball. On the other hand it may be a swishing sound that basketball players may recall when a shot has been made. If any of these sounds are heard, have the students repeat them mentally in their mind. It will help them to relive the experiences more fully.

- Is there something you can see that you remember?
- What did it look like?
- Was there a particular color associated with it?
- What was that color? Let the color flood your mind.
- Do you remember something you actually felt? It could be the roughness of a rock you were sitting on or the smoothness of a desk. It could be the warmth of the room or a fresh breeze on you face. It might be the pressure of a flexed muscle in your arms or legs. Let that feeling flood your mind.

Once the winning feeling has been established, sit and bathe in the emotions. The same feelings and the same physiological responses when the event actually occurred will return again. Get the emotional responses and keep them. After they have been experienced for a while, allow the students to drift out of them and relax. When relaxed, practice returning into the winning feeling state once again. This should be practiced several times so that movement in and out of the winning feeling state can occur at will.

Step Two

In order to be able to bring the winning feeling back easily, it can be anchored to a touch or word. The winning feeling could be anchored to the action of pinching the left ear lobe or rubbing the knuckle on one's little finger. The method is this. Have the students experience the winning feeling. When they are at the peak of their response and it can be felt as though they were actually experiencing the event, instruct them to rub the knuckle of their little finger. Repeat this several times to anchor the winning feeling to the rubbing of the little finger knuckle. After several sessions, they should be able to put themselves into their winning feeling state without any conscious effort other than rubbing their finger.

One of the advantages to anchoring the winning feeling to a response that isn't conspicuous is to enable a person to put himself into the winning feeling state without the effort of thinking and consciously going through the whole process earlier discussed.

Talk about control! Any gesture or action to anchor the winning feeling can be used. For example, rubbing or pinching the skin on the back of one's hand is effective. Keeping the response inconspicuous has the advantage of a person being able to get the winning feeling without anyone around being aware of what is taking place. The winning

feeling will be under the student's control. A peak physiological arousal state can be summoned at will so that each
student will be psychologically prepared for peak
performance in any upcoming challenge.

It is important to remember that students with poor self-
esteem will not be able to rely on their Reticular Activating
System to secrete the neuro-transmitters required to
physiologically prepare them for a challenging experience. By
learning to bring the winning feeling up at will puts the
students in control of their own peak states. Students must
learn to recall the winning feeling at will and then apply their
specific unique stimulus to anchor the feeling to that stimulus.
When this association is completed, students can activate the
winning feeling any time. Once learned, life becomes more
controllable. Life no longer is reactive, but proactive. A
growing sense of empowerment develops increasing self-
esteem.

Teaching students this skill gives them a sense of control
of their environment, a sense that they can take the initiative
to make decisions effecting their life without relying on
others. The weakness inherent in positive thinking books and
motivational workshops is that their influence is, for the most
part, short lived. However, learning how to bring up the
winning feeling at will and anchoring it to a specific stimulus,
permits students to practice the techniques, perfect them and
be able to see the positive results of their actions. They will
experience a growing sense of control and be internally
motivated to practice the technique as a life skill.

Step Three

The Anchoring Method

The next stage in the process involves linking the winning
feeling to specific situations or challenges. Life's hurdles face

all of us. Our past experiences with these hurdles have been frequently linked or associated with strong negative emotions. This can be problematic! The fear of failure or the fear of ridicule can cause individuals to feel inadequate thereby lowering their self-esteem and reducing the production of Neuro-transmitters in the brain. The cycle continues. Poor self-esteem leads to a low production of neuro-transmitters which leads to low functioning behavior which in turn reinforces the negative image leading back to poor self-esteem. (See Spiraling Results of Failure, pg. 14)

Once students can recall the WINNING FEELING at will, they are ready to anchor the feeling to a new behavior to be attempted or modified. New behaviors are often uncomfortable for students either because they have attached negative emotions to the behavior in the past or, simply because the behavior is new to them.

Consider the situation of exam anxiety so common to many students. Students need to put themselves into situations in which they would like to improve. They need to see themselves behaving the way they would like to behave and at the same time feeling the emotions of the WINNING FEELING state. What is required is to get students into a WINNING FEELING state that exudes confidence, creativity and success. Once in that state, a unique stimulus is anchored to that feeling so it can be recalled at will. Eventually with enough practice they can get into that state simply by doing their unique stimulus. After many sessions they will gradually change their Belief Systems by anchoring the Winning Feeling with new behaviors (see pg. 9 (chart)). Our Belief System was developed with a great deal of emotions. Therefore, strong emotions need to be included in any program to change the way we see ourselves.

Vivid visualizations (see Chapter 7) anchored to the Winning Feeling are the key skills to changing personal behaviors. Once students are able to visualize themselves performing in a situation with less anxiety or improved performance, then they should begin to associate the way they feel with their new performance. When they are at the peak of their emotions and they are reacting physically and mentally the way they would be if they really were in that state, apply a specific unique stimulus that will now be anchored to the Winning Feeling. In order to facilitate the anchoring, it is important to get the individuals to use all of their senses, both mentally and kinesthetically. Students should be asked if they hear any sounds or can they talk like they would (tone of voice, rapidity of speech, etc.) while they are in their Winning Feeling. Can they describe what they see? Are there any specific colors that dominate the scene? Can they actually feel anything? The texture of an object or the responses from their body. They could be asked to assume the posture of a confident person. Move and breathe like a confident person. Using all of these resources has greater influence on altering the individuals' Belief System and synaptically burns the new behavior into their brains.

Keys to Successful Anchoring

The four keys to successful anchoring or bonding the winning feeling (the emotions or feeling of power, control or competency) to specific situations (a mental visualization or the actual situation) are as follows:

1) The person must be completely involved—mind and body relaxed.

2) The specific unique stimulus must be provided at the peak of the experience.

3) The stimulus should be unique and one that can be done without drawing attention to oneself—pinching the skin on the back of the hand or rubbing the knuckle on your left baby finger.

4) In order for the anchor to be effective, it must be done exactly the same way each time...consistency counts!

It is extremely important that the four keys to successful anchoring are replicated exactly according to the format stated. Those who recall watching Debbie Thomas skate in the Olympics in Calgary, may remember that much was said about the way she felt, her heavy schedule and the fact that she had not as much preparation as she needed. The television cameras were trained on her to dramatize her entrance and the last minute instructions given to her from her sports psychologist. He held her hands and gave her encouragement emphasizing his points by pumping her hands up and down. All of this advice, although well meaning would have little effect in putting Miss Thomas into the correct mental state unless this motivating technique was used with her all the time and she was accustomed to responding to this technique.

Her skating performance was poor. Her winning feeling was probably not anchored to the way in which the coach was speaking to her. Varying the specific stimulus only slightly will render the stimulus ineffective. Consistency counts!

Let's do a simple basic exercise to anchor self-confidence. This will be written as if a teacher was speaking to a student who wanted to change. Let's begin:

"Stand up and think of a time when you were totally confident. Put your body in the same physiology. Feel the goose bumps or the rush of adrenaline serge through your body. Stand the way you did." (Apply the specific unique stimulus.)

"Breathe the way you would if you were totally confident." (Apply the Specific Unique Stimulus.)

"Speak in a confident tone." (Apply the Specific Unique Stimulus.)

Repeat this five or six times until you can easily move into that specific state.

If students do not have any experiences that can be called upon, imagining how they think they would act if they had confidence may be helpful. This technique applies to entering any desired state. Some negatively programmed individuals may not have experienced any peak performance states in the past. Role modeling heroes from television or the movies may act as a suitable substitute. When this occurs, be sure that the individuals visualize everything about the hero until they can begin to feel the state they want to be in. Then make a link to a specific stimulus. Repeating the procedure several times having the students stimulate themselves several times with their specific stimulus, begins to alter their Belief System, the first step to becoming who they want to be.

To increase the power of an anchor, several successful experiences need to be associated with the anchor. This procedure reinforces the association giving it more strength. This in effect is the same as providing a history of experience to the individual. One's BELIEF SYSTEM took years to develop. By providing many positive experiences in a short time using a combination of the WINNING FEELING and visualization, an accelerated history is being provided to reinforce a new and developing BELIEF SYSTEM. It must be emphasized that the WINNING FEELING is so much more powerful as a change agent when there is strong emotion present as well. When in the WINNING FEELING state, if students can feel the emotions of excitement, the emotions of being successful and powerful, they are well on their way to making changes that will be permanent. If lapses do occur, the skills necessary to reinforce the links between where they are currently performing and where they want to be will be available to them. Thus, there is a need for a string of successful experiences in close succession. The many positive experiences reinforce the Belief Systems and the neural patterns are more firmly established so that this becomes a new way of processing experiences. The more often a WINNING FEELING state is repeated successfully, the more powerful will be the association which establishes a new pattern of thinking, a new filter through which to view life.

In his book *Ultimate Power,* Tony Robbins suggests anchoring a different skill on a different knuckle. For example, creativity could be anchored to one knuckle and decision-making to another. The limit is based on the skills the individuals feel they need. Once the decision is made as to which skills are desired, a series of reinforcements is done to synaptically burn the new patterns of thinking into the neurology of the brain. Eventually squeezing any of the specific knuckles and adding the auditory sound will get the students into their desired states immediately.

A problem in neural reprogramming is dealing with negative associations. If a person does not feel comfortable with a situation, it may be difficult to change the way he feels about it. One of the most successful approaches to change perception is to have the students associate the negative stimuli with a new positive response. In other words, have the negative stimuli that caused nervousness, feelings of incompetency, and general overall lack of control generate feeling of control, power and competency. For example, students who feel they are poor exam writers and forget information will claim that it's almost as if there were a strong magnetic field at the entrance of the exam room that erases their minds as they pass through it. When they leave the exam room they often remember what should have been put down or how they should have calculated the math question. These students see the exam room, the desk, the exam paper, the feeling of the pencil in their hands, the pressure of the desk on their seats and the noise of the room. These stimuli are all anchored to poor writing skills, poor memory, poor thinking, and general incompetency. As a person causing change, the teacher's role is to make all of the stimuli that triggered negative responses in the future trigger positive responses. Reframing of the situation is needed! When states of competency occur, they must be anchored to the external stimuli of the whole exam room and atmosphere. The result will be that the new association to the exam room, desk, paper, etc,....will be feelings of competency and confidence. The stimuli that caused panic and fear now become associated with confidence and competence.

Teachers can create anchors (association) between their subject areas and a comfortable atmosphere in the class. A classroom that is relaxed in which learning, with no fear of ridicule for poor answers, where tests are designed so students can demonstrate success will develop associations of comfortableness and general well being for students. Students will be excited about being there and will be more likely to work independently and competently. They may not remember the specific lesson but they will remember the comfortable feelings they had and feel good about school and learning. This is laying the foundation for future feelings of success associated with school and learning.

Summary

Belief systems develop in individuals as a result of their experiences. The degree to which we hold onto these beliefs is directly proportional to the emotional intensity attached to them. The greater the emotions attached to the belief, the stronger it is held. In order to cause change, new ways of behaving must be visualized. Along with visualization, strong positive emotions (winning feelings) must be linked or anchored together. These strong emotions will allow for more permanent change. Once individuals can get into winning feeling states (emotionally and physically), these states are anchored to specific unique stimuli. When the unique specific stimuli are called upon, they immediately put the individual into the desired states. This allows them to function competently and confidently. These new ways of behaving may be further entrenched through reinforcement of several positive experiences, one after the other to neurologically provide another history causing more permanent change. Different parts of the body (unique stimuli) can be anchored to specific states and competencies the person desires. Stimuli that cause negative responses can be reassociated with positive responses. Stimuli that once caused problems can now become associated with positive traits like competency and confidence.

SUMMARY CHAPTER 8

1. The Winning Feeling is an intense emotional high that accompanies a sense of accomplishment, a sense of being someone special or a sense of being at ease with oneself.

2. Improved performance can occur when we attach

feelings associated with past successes to new behavior. This process is called anchoring to significant emotional events. It can also be accomplished by reframing a behavior to a new context.

3. By attaching desired performance to the winning feeling, and visualizing ourselves performing in the new way, we establish new engrams or patterns of thought that are synaptically linked. Once established, the new patterns will emerge reflexively in the future. Engrams are our blue print for new behavior. It is through this process that new behavior leading to an improved self-concept can be realized.

Bibliography

Botterill, Cal. "Goal Setting and Athletic Development," *SPORTS,* Coaching Association of Canada, Ottawa, 1983.

Botterill, C. and Winston, G. "Psychological Skill Development," *Science Periodical on Research and Technology in Sport,* Coaching Association of Canada, Aug. 1984.

Chevalier, N. "Understanding the Imagery and Mental Rehearsal Processes in Athletics," *Science Periodical on Research and Technology in Sport,* Coaching Association of Canada, Oct. 1988.

Ciglen, L. and Ciglen, L.A. "Encouraging Self-Esteem," *OPSTF News,* October 1989, p. 10-13.

Fanning, Patrick. "Visualization for Change," *New Harbinger Publications,* Inc. Oakland, Ca., 1988.

Gauron, E.F. "Mental Training for Peak Performance," *Sport Science Associates,* Lansing, N.Y., 1985.

Gill, D.L. "Psychological Dynamics of Sport," *Human Kinetics Publishers,* Champaigne, Ill., 1986.

Green, E.E. and Green, A.M. "Striate and Autonomic Self Regulation: Biofeedback and Yoga," *Science Periodical on Research and Technology in Sport,* Coaching Association of Canada, July, 1987.

Harris, D.V. and Harris, B.L. "Sports Psychology: Mental Skills for Physical People," *Leisure Press,* Champaigne, Ill. 1984.

Joy, J. "Mirror, Mirror on the Wall: Self-Evaluation for Peak Performance," *Science Periodical on Research and Technology in Sport,* Coaching Association of Canada, Jan. 1987.

Kearns, J. "The Impact of Systematic Feedback on Student's Self-Esteem," Ph.D. diss., University of Alberta, Edmonton, 1987.

Krueger, K.A. "Practical Sports Psychology for Coaches," *Science Periodical on Research and Technology in Sport*, Coaching Association of Canada, Dec. 1987.

Kubistant, T. "Performing Your Best," *Life Enhancement Publications*, Champaigne, Ill. 1986.

Lakein, A. "How to Get Control of Your Time and Your Life," New York: Peter Wyden, 1973.

LeBoeuf, M. "Imagineering," *Berkley Books*, New York, 1986.

Loehr, J.E. and McLaughlin, P.J. "Mentally Tough," *Totem Books*, Toronto, 1986.

Mackay, H. "Swim with the Sharks Without Being Eaten Alive,"*Ivy Books*, New York, 1988.

Maltz, M. "Psycho-cybernetics," *Prentice-Hall*, New York, 1960.

Orlick, T. "In Pursuit of Excellence," Coaching Association of Canada, Ottawa, 1980.

Orlick, T. "In Pursuit of Excellence," Second Edition, *Leisure Press*, Champaigne, Ill. 1990.

Orlick, T. and Partington, J. "Excellence Through Mental Training," *Science Periodical on Research and Technology in Sport,* Coaching Association of Canada, May 1986.

Ostrander, S. and Ostrander, L. "Super-Learning," *Laurel-Confucian Press Book*, New York, 1979.

Otto, H. "More Joy in Your Marriage," *Simon & Schuster*, Toronto, 1971.

Pennington, S. "Healing Yourself--Understanding How Your Mind Can Heal Your Body," *McGraw-Hill Ryerson Limited*, Toronto, 1988.

Porter, K. and Foster, J. "The Mental Athlete," *Ballantine Books*, New York, 1986.

Rushall, B. "Psyching in Sport," *Pelham Books:London*, 1979.

Ulich, E. "Some experiments on the function of mental training in the acquisition of motor skills," *Ergonomics*, 1967, 10, 411-419.

Waitley, D. "Seeds of Greatness," *Simon and Schuster, Inc.*, New York, 1983.

Waitley, D. "The Winner's Edge," *Berkley Books*, New York, 1985.

Waitley, D. "The Psychology of Winning," *Berkley Books*, New York, 1985.

Waitley, D. "The Double Win," *Berkley Books*, New York, 1986.

Wattenburg, M.W. and Clifford, C. "Relationships of self-concepts to beginning achievement in reading," *Child Development*, 35:461-467, 1967.

Wilson, V.E. and Bird, E.I. "Understanding Self-Regulation Training in Sport," *Science Periodical on Research and Technology in Sport*, Coaching Association of Canada, Oct.1982.

RELATED REFERENCES

Bell, K. "Coaching Excellence," *Keel Publications,* Austin, Texas, 1985.

Benson, H. "The Relaxation Response," *Avon Books*, New York, 1976.

Benson, H. "Your Maximum Mind," *Avon Books*, New York, 1987.

Csikszentmahalyi, M. "Flow: The Psychology of Optimal Experience," *Harper and Row,* Publishers, Toronto, 1990.

Denning, M. and Phillips, O. "Creative Visualization," *Llewellyn Publications*, St. Paul, Minn., 1989

Glasser, W. "Positive Addiction," *Harper and Row,* Publishers, New York, 1976.

Harris, D.V. and Harris, B.L. "Sports Psychology: Mental Skills for Physical People," *Leisure Press*, Champaign, Ill., 1984.

Helmstetter, S. "What to Say When You Talk to Yourself," *Pocket Books*, New York, 1986.

Helmstetter, S. "The Self-Talk Solution," *Pocket Books*, New York, 1987.

Hill, N. and Clement Stone, W. "Success through a Positive Mental Attitude," *Pocket Books*, Toronto, 1977.

Levinson, H. "Executive Stress," *Mentor Book*, Scarborough, Ont., 1975.

MacKay, H. "Swim With the Sharks Without Being Eaten Alive," *Ivy Books*, New York, 1988.

Martens, R. "Coaches Guide to Sport Psychology," *Human Kinetics Publishers*, Inc., Champaign, Ill., 1988.

Noe, J.R. "Peak Performance Principles for High Achievers," *Berkley Books*, New York, 1986.

Orlick, T. "Coaches Training Manual to Psyching For Sport," *Leisure Press,* Champaign, Ill., 1986.

Orlick, T. "Psyching for Sport: Mental Training for Athletes," *Leisure Press,* Champaign, Ill., 1986.

Orlick, T. and Partington, J. "Psyched: Inner Views of Winning," Coaching Association of Canada, Ottawa, 1986.

Orlick, T., Partington, J., and Salmela, J.H. (Ed.) "Mental Training for Coaches and Athletes," Coaching Association of Canada, 1983.

Tracy, B. and Youngs, B.B. "Achievement, Happiness, Popularity and Success," *The Phoenix Educational Foundation,* Solana Beach, Cal., 1988.

Waitley, D. "The Winner's Edge," *Berkley Books*, New York, 1980.

Index